C++ Data Structures

Third Edition

A Laboratory Course

D1591894

Stefan Brandle
Taylor University

Jonathan Geisler
Taylor University

James Robergé

David Whittington
Filtro Systems, Inc.

JONES AND BARTLETT PUBLISHERS
Sudbury, Massachusetts
BOSTON   TORONTO   LONDON   SINGAPORE

World Headquarters

Jones and Bartlett Publishers
40 Tall Pine Drive
Sudbury, MA 01776
978-443-5000
info@jbpub.com
www.jbpub.com

Jones and Bartlett Publishers
Canada
6339 Ormindale Way
Mississauga, Ontario L5V 1J2
Canada

Jones and Bartlett Publishers
International
Barb House, Barb Mews
London W6 7PA
United Kingdom

Jones and Bartlett's books and products are available through most bookstores and online booksellers. To contact Jones and Bartlett Publishers directly, call 800-832-0034, fax 978-443-8000, or visit our website www.jbpub.com.

Substantial discounts on bulk quantities of Jones and Bartlett's publications are available to corporations, professional associations, and other qualified organizations. For details and specific discount information, contact the special sales department at Jones and Bartlett via the above contact information or send an email to specialsales@jbpub.com.

Production Credits
Acquisitions Editor: Tim Anderson
Production Director: Amy Rose
Editorial Assistant: Melissa Elmore
Senior Marketing Manager: Andrea DeFronzo
Manufacturing Buyer: Therese Connell
Composition: Northeast Compositors
Cover Design: Kate Ternullo
Cover Image: © Cocota Anca/ShutterStock, Inc.
Printing and Binding: Courier Stoughton
Cover Printing: Courier Stoughton

6048
Printed in the United States of America
12 11 10 09 08   10 9 8 7 6 5 4 3 2 1

To Christina, Anna, and Esther, for giving me the time to work on this.
 —Stefan Brandle

To the women in my life. Thanks for the great deal of understanding with so little payback time.
 —Jonathan Geisler

To Michael, for letting me share in his creativity.
 —James Robergé

To my family and to Melissa.
 —David Whittington

contents

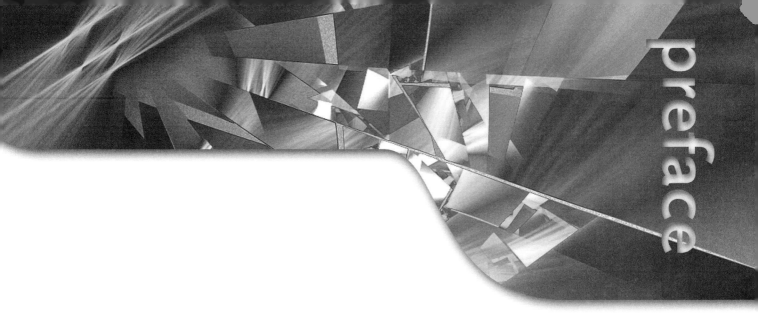

Preface to the Third Edition

We have used James Robergé's laboratory manual for eight years at Taylor University. The approach and style of the original manual made it an extremely effective teaching tool. In 2002, we were given the privilege of updating the first edition to reflect changes in C++ and to add some new material.

It is now time for a third edition. Perhaps most significantly, all the worksheet pages—which comprised a high percentage of the book—were moved into a set of online supplements that instructors and students can print as needed. The appendix material is now widely available online from multiple sources.

We discovered that many of those using the book are now using it for more advanced courses such as Data Structures and Algorithms. A major reason for this is that many universities have switched the second computer science course (CS2, sometimes also called Data Structures) from C++ to Java. Given that the target audience has shifted somewhat, and that students using the lab book have probably already encountered Object-Oriented Programming, we chose to increase the level of C++ and data structure sophistication. However, we ensured that the book is still very usable for CS2—which is where we continue to use it.

Aspects of the second edition were out of date because of changes in the C++ language. Also, compilers have caught up enough with newer C++ standards that we can safely use some of the features that either did not exist previously, or were not reliably supported by enough common compilers. For example, the use of `typename` instead of `class` in templates.

Our goal to be true to Jim Robergé's original vision of the laboratory experience remains, but we also recognize that the book is no longer necessarily used with the classic closed lab. As a consequence, we modified our nomenclature. For instance, In-Lab Exercises are now called Programming Exercises. Post-Lab Exercises are now called Analysis Exercises. These can still be used as in-lab/post-lab exercises with a closed lab, but the naming more accurately reflects the reality that these labs can be used equally well as regular weekly programming assignments in a non-laboratory course.

Overview of Changes

Each chapter has been organized into Objectives, ADT Overview, C++ Concepts Overview, ADT Specification, Implementation Notes, Compilation Directions, and Testing. Then, there are three Programming Exercises and two Analysis Exercises.

We also made the following significant changes:

- Introduced a configuration file, *config.h*, that allows students to control which ADT extensions are used by the test program. We feel that this method is cleaner and a better example for students than the laborious uncommenting and recommenting that was required.
- Error handling is streamlined: `bad_alloc` exceptions have been removed.
- The word `class` in templates has been replaced by the new keyword `typename`. The keyword `typename` is intuitively more self-explanatory and is not as overloaded as `class`.
- For the linked data structures where we had external "Node" classes, they have become inner classes. Although inner classes add a small amount of syntax, it gets away from the issues of forward declarations for mutually referring classes. This represents better object-oriented design and we avoid the use of declaring class `friends`.
- Copy constructors and overloaded assignment operators are now required for every ADT implementation.
- The `isFull` operation has been removed from linked data structures where it is not required for compatibility with the array-based version. We do this because determining whether dynamic memory is exhausted is a fruitless and inefficient exercise. In reality, C++ provides an exception mechanism to deal with this issue.
- More sophisticated use of templates is presented. Template specialization is introduced in the Expression Tree. Default template types and template parameters are introduced in the Heap.
- Lab order has been changed to be compatible with the order in the largest number of current textbooks. The singly-linked list was moved up to Lab 5 right after the two array-based lists; the expression tree is now before the binary search tree; the string lab was moved to Lab 1; and the BlogEntry ADT—the only new lab—is Lab 2.

Note: We still do not use STL in this book (except for one example in the Performance Analysis lab). However, the STL implementation of a data structure could be substituted for the student's implementation in necessary situations.

To the Student

Objectives

The courses that we enjoyed most when we were students were those that emphasized design. In design-oriented courses, we used the concepts taught to solve practical problems. The process of applying ideas made it easier to understand them and their application in a real-world setting.

This emphasis on learning by doing is used throughout this book. In each laboratory, you will explore a particular data structure by implementing it. As you create an implementation, you will learn how the data structure works and how it can be applied. The resulting implementation is a working piece of software that you can later use in laboratories and programming projects.

Organization of the Laboratories

Each laboratory consists of three parts: Basic Implementation and Testing, Programming Exercises, and Analysis Exercises. The Basic Implementation section explains the specific Abstract Data Type (ADT), introduces the new C++ concepts, describes the ADT's properties, explains implementation details that you need to know, and then guides you through testing your implementation. In the three Programming Exercises, the first exercise is usually to apply the data structure you created to the solution of a problem. The remaining two exercises usually apply or extend the concepts introduced in the Basic Implementation. The last part of each laboratory, the Analysis Exercise, is an assignment in which you analyze a data structure in terms of its efficiency or use.

Your instructor will specify which exercises you need to complete for each laboratory and when they are due. You are encouraged to use the cover sheet provided with the online laboratory worksheets to keep track of the exercises you have been assigned. Implementation testing is very important—probably just as important a step as implementing the ADT—and should not be skipped.

Student Resources

The authors have compiled a set of worksheets, interactive tools to test and debug your work, and "starter kits" containing data, partial solution shells, and other supporting routines for each of your labs. These tools are available for download at the Jones and Bartlett lab book website http://www.jbpub.com/catalog/9780763755645.

To the Instructor

Objectives

When James Robergé was first given the opportunity to introduce laboratories into his data structures course, he jumped at the chance. He saw laboratories as a way of involving students as active, creative partners in the learning process. By making the laboratories the focal point of the course, he sought to immerse his students in the course material. The goal of each lab is still to challenge students to exercise their creativity (in both programming and analysis) while at the same time providing the structure, feedback, and support that they need to meet the challenge. This manual is the product of years of experimentation and refinement working toward this objective.

Organization of the Laboratories

In the initial development of these labs, an attempt was made to shoehorn the creative process into a series of two-hour laboratories. The result was a pressure cooker that challenged everyone, but helped no one. In experimenting with solutions to this problem, James Robergé developed a laboratory framework that retains the creative element but shifts the time-intensive aspects outside the laboratory period. Within this structure, each laboratory includes three parts: Basic Implementation and Testing, Programming Exercises, and Analysis Exercises.

The Basic Implementation section explains the specific Abstract Data Type (ADT), introduces the new C++ concepts, describes the ADT's properties, explains implementation details that the student needs to know, and then guides the student through testing his/her implementation. In the three Programming Exercises, the first exercise is usually to apply the data structure to the solution of a problem. The remaining two exercises usually apply or extend the concepts introduced in the Basic Implementation. The last part of each laboratory, the Analysis Exercise, is an assignment which analyzes a data structure in terms of its efficiency or use.

Basic Implementation

The Basic Implementation exercise is intended as a homework assignment that links the lecture with the laboratory period. Students explore and create on their own and at their own pace. Their goal is to synthesize the information they learn in lectures with material from their textbook to produce a working piece of software, usually an implementation of an abstract data type (ADT). The implementation assignment—including a review of the relevant lecture and textbook materials—typically takes four to five hours to complete. We have tried to include all necessary discussions of new C++ material, implementation details, special compilation directions, and testing instructions. You should give students specific instructions for compilation in your laboratory environment.

An interactive, command-driven test program is provided for each laboratory, along with a text-based visualization routine that allows students to see changes in the content and organization of a data structure. This part of the assignment provides an opportunity for students to receive feedback on their basic implementation and to resolve any difficulties they might have encountered. It should take students approximately one hour to finish this exercise. Students are often tempted to skimp on the testing, resulting in poorly implemented submissions. Requiring students to complete and submit the test plans in the online worksheets can significantly improve the quality of submissions.

Programming Exercises

This section takes place during the actual laboratory period (assuming you are using a closed laboratory setting). Each lab contains three exercises, and each exercise has a distinct role. In Exercise 1, students apply the software they developed in the Basic Implementation to a real-world problem that has been honed to its essentials to fit comfortably within the closed laboratory environment. The last two exercises stress programming by extending the data structure, and provide a capstone to the basic implementation. Exercise 1 can be completed in approximately one and a half hours. Exercises 2 and 3 can take as much as one hour each to complete, but students who did the initial work thoroughly have a better understanding and can finish more quickly.

Most students will not be able to complete all these programming exercises within a typical closed laboratory period. We have provided a range of exercises so that you can select those that best suit your laboratory environment and your students' needs.

Analysis Exercises

The last phase of each laboratory is a set of two homework assignments in which students analyze the efficiency or utility of a given data structure. Each Analysis Exercise should take roughly thirty minutes to complete. Assuming a closed laboratory structure, one or both could be done following the laboratory period.

Using the Three-Part Organization in Your Laboratory Environment

The term *laboratory* is used by computer science instructors to denote a broad range of environments. One group of students in a data structures course, for example, may attend a closed two-hour laboratory; at the same time, another group of students may take the class in a televised format and "attend" an open laboratory. In developing this manual, we have preserved the first edition's efforts to create a laboratory format suitable for a variety of open and closed laboratory settings. How you use the organization depends on your laboratory environment.

Two-Hour Closed Laboratory

Basic Implementation
We expect the students attending a two-hour closed laboratory to make a good-faith effort to complete the basic implementation exercise before coming to the lab. Their work need not be perfect, but their effort must be real (roughly 80% correct). We ask our students to complete the test plans and to begin testing and debugging their implementation work prior to coming to lab (as part of the 80% correct guideline).

Programming Exercises
We use the first hour of the laboratory period to resolve any problems the students might have experienced in completing the Basic Implementation and Testing. Our intention is to give constructive feedback so that students leave the lab with a working implementation—a significant accomplishment on their part.

During the second hour, we have students complete one of the programming exercises in order to reinforce the concepts learned in the basic implementation. You can choose the exercise by section or by student, or you can let the students decide which one to complete.

Students leave the lab having received feedback on their basic implementation and additional programming exercise work. You need not rigidly enforce the hourly divisions; a mix of activities keeps everyone interested and motivated.

Analysis Exercises
After the lab, the students complete one (or both) of the analysis exercises and turn it in during their next lab period.

One-Hour Closed Laboratory

Basic Implementation
If we have only one hour for the closed laboratory, we ask students to complete all of the Basic Implementation and Testing before they come to the lab. This work is turned in at the start of the period.

Programming Exercises
During the laboratory period, the students complete one of the additional programming exercises.

Analysis Exercises
Again, the students complete one or both of the analysis exercises and submit it during their next lab period.

Open Laboratory

In an open laboratory setting, we have the students complete the Basic Implementation and Testing exercises, one of the additional programming exercises, and one or both of the analysis exercises. You can stagger the submission of these exercises throughout the week or have students turn in the entire laboratory as a unit.

Student Preparation

This manual assumes that students have a background in either Java or C++. The first laboratory introduces classes and the use of classes to implement a simple ADT. Succeeding laboratories introduce more complex C++ language features (dynamic memory allocation, templates, inheritance, and so forth) in the context of data structures that use these features.

Order of Topics

All instructors cover the course material in the order that they believe best suits their students' needs. To give instructors flexibility in the order of presentation, we have made the individual laboratories as independent of one another as possible. At a minimum, we recommend beginning with the following sequence of laboratories:

Laboratory 1 (*Text ADT*)
> Introduces the implementation of an ADT using C++ classes and a number of foundational features, including constructors, destructors, basic dynamic memory allocation, and operator overloading. Depending on the student background, you may choose to implement this over the course of two weeks.

Laboratory 2 (*BlogEntry ADT*)
> Continues the overview of significant C++ features. Introduces member initialization, exceptions, static methods, class composition, and extending `iostream` functionality.

Laboratory 3 (*Array Implementation of the List ADT*)
> Introduces templates and prepares students for inheritance.

Laboratory 5 (*Singly-Linked Implementation of the List ADT*)
> Introduces linked lists and inner classes.

We have placed the performance evaluation laboratory at the end of the book (Laboratory 13), because in our experience, we have found that everyone covers this topic at a different time. Rather than bury it in the middle of the manual, we have placed it at the end so that you can include it where it best serves you and your students' needs, be that early in the semester, in the middle, or toward the end.

ADT Implementation

The laboratories are designed to complement a variety of approaches to implementing each ADT. All ADT definitions stress the use of data abstraction and generic data elements. As a result, you can adapt them with minimal effort to suit different implementation strategies.

For each ADT, class declarations that frame an implementation of the ADT are given as part of the corresponding basic implementation exercise. This declaration framework is also used in the visualization function that accompanies the laboratory. Should you elect to adopt a somewhat different implementation strategy, you need only make minor changes to the data members in the class declarations and corresponding modifications to the visualization routine. You do not need to change anything else in either the supplied software or the laboratory text itself.

Differences Between the Manual and Your Text

We have found that variations in style between the approaches used in the textbook and the laboratory manual discourage students from simply copying material from the textbook. Having to make changes, however slight, encourages them to examine in more detail how a given implementation works.

Combining the Laboratories with Programming Projects

One of our goals in designing these laboratories was to enable students to produce the laboratory code that they can use again as part of larger, more applications-oriented programming projects. The ADTs the students develop in the basic implementation exercises provide a solid foundation for such projects. Reusing the material that they created in the laboratory frees students to focus on the application they are developing. More important, they see in concrete terms—their time and effort—the value of such essential software engineering concepts as code reuse, data abstraction, and object-oriented programming.

The first extra programming exercise in each lab is usually an application problem based on the material covered in the basic implementation for that laboratory. These exercises provide an excellent starting point for programming projects. Free-form projects are also possible.

Student Resources

Challenging students is easy; helping them to meet a challenge is not. The student resources found at the Jones and Bartlett website for the book include a set of software tools that assist students in developing ADT implementations. The tools provide students with the means for testing an ADT implementation using simple keyboard commands and for visualizing the resulting data structure using ASCII text on a standard text display. Additional files containing data, partial solution shells, other supporting routines, and online worksheets are also available for download at http://www.jbpub.com/catalog/9780763755645.

Instructor's Resources

An instructor's solutions kit is available for download at the publisher's website. Solutions to all of the basic implementation and extra programming exercises are included. To register, please visit: http://www.jbpub.com/catalog/9780763755645.

We have been using online unit testing technology to automate the submission, assessment, and feedback generation for student labs. If you are interested, please contact Stefan Brandle (sbrandle@css.taylor.edu) for details. In addition, if you have questions, discover errors, etc., please feel free to send an email.

Acknowledgments

Writing this type of lab manual is an "iceberg" project—much of the work goes into the implementation of a programming infrastructure that is only somewhat visible on the printed page. We owe many thanks to James Robergé for the vision that inspired the lab. We are also indebted to all the reviewers, editors, and publication teams who helped with make the first, second, and third editions reality. In particular, we wish to thank the current team at Jones and Bartlett for their patience and work: Tim Anderson, Amy Rose, and Melissa Elmore.

Additionally, our family members are always owed a big thank you for supporting us kindly throughout the process.

S.B.

Text ADT

In this laboratory, you

- are introduced to the concept of an Abstract Data Type (ADT).

- implement an ADT using a C++ class.

- use the C++ operators `new` and `delete` to dynamically allocate and deallocate memory.

- learn the C++ mechanisms for implementing classes correctly and efficiently.

- create a program that performs lexical analysis using your new Text data type.

- examine the problems with the standard C string representation.

ADT Overview

The purpose of this laboratory is for you to explore how you can use C++ classes to implement an abstract data type (ADT). In this laboratory, you will implement your own string type, the Text class.

When computers were first introduced, they were popularly characterized as giant calculating machines. This characterization ignores the fact that computers are equally adept at manipulating other forms of information, including sequences of symbols called strings. Text is a type of string that is composed of human-readable characters. In this lab we will be working with text.

C++ provides a set of predefined, or "built-in," data types (e.g., int, char, and float). Each of these predefined types has a set of operations associated with it. You use these operations to manipulate variables of a given type. For example, type int supports the basic arithmetic and relational operators, as well as a number of numerical functions (abs and div, etc.). These predefined data types provide a foundation on which you construct more sophisticated data types, types that are collections of related data items, rather than individual data items. Each of the user defined data types in this book will be discussed in two steps. First, we describe them as ADTs (abstract data types). An ADT is the description of a set of data items and of the operations that can be performed on that data. The "abstract" part means that the data type is described independent of any implementation details. Second, we discuss implementation details for turning the ADT description into a usable language-specific data structure. You will implement each ADT by writing one or more C++ classes that make it possible to instantiate actual C++ objects—variables of the user-defined data type—that meet the ADT specifications.

When specifying an ADT, you begin by describing the data items that are in the ADT. You describe how the ADT data items are organized to form the ADT's structure. In the case of the Text ADT, the data items are the letters associated with a text string and the structure is linear: the entries are arranged in the same order as they would appear in written form.

Having specified the data items and the structure of the ADT, you then define how the ADT can be used by specifying the operations that are associated with the ADT. For each operation, you specify what conditions must be true before the operation can be applied (its preconditions, or requirements) as well as what conditions will be true after the operation has completed (its postconditions, or results). The following Text ADT specification includes operations to create and initialize a Text object, assign text to it, compare it to other Text objects, and retrieve the letters at specific positions within the Text object.

C++ Concepts Overview

Many important C++ concepts are introduced in this lab. In this section, we briefly describe each.

Constructors: This is a member function that is automatically run to initialize new objects when they are created. If each C++ class has an appropriate constructor, it will guarantee that all objects of that class are initialized before the programmer can do anything else with the object, thus ensuring that the programmer will always be working with properly initialized data. Like overloaded functions, there can be multiple constructors provided that each has a unique combination of parameter types (the function's signature). To be safe, all C++ classes should have one or more constructors.

Destructor: This is a member function that automatically runs when an object is destroyed. The destructor is responsible for doing any object "clean up" that needs to happen before the object is destroyed. The destructor's most important responsibility in C++ is to ensure that any memory the object borrowed from the memory manager gets returned correctly. Object destruction happens implicitly when the object goes out of scope, or as a result of the programmer explicitly deleting an object.

Dynamic memory allocation: It is quite common to need a block of memory of a specific size—typically an array—at runtime. In C++, the code requests this memory from the memory management routines by using the `new` keyword. When the memory block is no longer needed, it is returned to the dynamic memory pool by using the `delete` keyword. Forgetting to return dynamically allocated memory leads to a serious problem called a memory leak. Any class that performs dynamic memory allocation needs a destructor to help return the memory when the object gets destroyed.

Class protection and access mechanisms: Data and member functions in C++ classes can be protected from access outside the class by declaring them in one of three sections of the class: public, private, and protected. Anything declared in the `public` section is freely accessible from anywhere outside the class. The object-oriented programming (OOP) philosophy is that data and member functions should be public only on a "need to be public" basis, so they should only be placed in the public section if they really need to be there. Data is almost never declared as public. Items in the `private` section are accessible only to member functions within that class. Member functions and data in the `protected` section are treated as private, except that classes that are derived from the given class (through inheritance) are given access to anything in the protected section. C++ also allows the use of `friend` to let a class give a function or another class access to its contents. The use of `friend` will be discussed later when it is needed.

Operator overloading: C++ knows what to do when it sees operators used with predefined data types, but it generally does not know what to do with the user-defined data types and doesn't even try. And when it does try, the results are often not what the programmer intended. To solve the behavior problem, C++ allows a class to redefine the meaning of an operator used in the context of an object of that class. Examples include the '<', '=', '==', '[]', and '+' operators.

Const protection: In C++, there are sometimes objects that may not be changed in a specific context. In those cases, the compiler needs to know whether calling a specific member function would illegally change the object. A member function can be declared to be a `const` function, meaning that running it does not cause changes to any of the object's data values. Additionally, a function parameter can be declared `const`, meaning that the function may not modify the parameter.

Text ADT Specification

Data items

A set of characters, excluding the null character.

Structure

The characters in a Text object are in sequential (or linear) order—that is, the characters follow one after the other from the beginning of a string to its end.

Operations

```
Text ( const char* charSeq = "" )
```

Requirements:
None

Results:
Conversion constructor and default constructor. Creates a Text object containing the character sequence in the array pointed to by `charSeq`. This constructor assumes that `charSeq` is a valid C-string terminated by the null character ('\0') and allocates enough memory for the characters in the array plus any delimiter that may be required by the implementation of the Text ADT.

```
Text ( const Text& other )
```

Requirements:
None

Results:
Copy constructor. Initializes the object to be an equivalent copy of `other`. This constructor is invoked automatically whenever a Text object is passed to a function using call by value, a function returns a Text object, or a Text object is initialized using another Text object.

```
void operator= ( const Text& other )
```

Requirements:
None

Results:
Assigns the value of `other` to this Text object.

```
~Text ()
```

Requirements:
None

Results:
Destructor. Deallocates (frees) the memory used for the implementation of the Text ADT.

```
int getLength () const
```

Requirements:
None

Results:
Returns the number of characters in the Text object (excluding the delimiter).

```
char operator [] ( int n ) const
```

Requirements:
None

Results:
Returns the nth character in the Text object—where the characters are numbered beginning with zero. If the object does not have an nth character, then it returns the null character.

```
void clear ()
```

Requirements:
None

Results:
Clears the Text object, thereby making it an empty Text object.

```
void showStructure () const
```

Requirements:
None

Results:
Outputs the characters in the Text object, as well as the delimiter. Note that this operation is intended for testing/debugging purposes only.

Implementation Notes

C-strings: C++ supports the manipulation of character data through the predefined data type `char` and the associated operations for the input, output, assignment, and comparison of characters. Most applications of character data require character sequences—or strings—rather than individual characters. A string can be represented in C++ using a one-dimensional array of characters. By convention, a string begins in array data item zero and is terminated by the null character, `'\0'`. (That is how C and early C++ represented strings. Although C++ now has a standard string class, many current programming APIs—Application Programming Interfaces—require a knowledge of the C-string representation.)

Representing a string as an array of characters terminated by a null suffers from several defects, including the following:

- The subscript operator (`[]`) does not check that the subscript lies within the boundaries of the string—or even within the boundaries of the array holding the string, for that matter.
- Strings are compared using functions that have far different calling conventions than the familiar relational operators (`==`, `<`, `>`, and so forth).
- The assignment operator (`=`) simply copies a pointer, not the character data it points to. The code fragment shown here, for example,

```
char *str1 = "data",
    *str2;
str2 = str1;
```

makes `str2` point to the array already pointed to by `str1`. It does not create a new array containing the string `"data"`. This results in changes to `str2` affecting `str1` since they share the array, and vice versa.

Either the length of a string must be declared at compile-time or a program must explicitly allocate and deallocate the memory used to store a string. Declaring the length of a string at compile-time is often impossible, or at least inefficient. Allocating and deallocating the memory used by a string dynamically (that is, at run-time) allows the string length to be set (or changed) as a program executes. Unfortunately, it is very easy for a programmer to forget to include code to deallocate memory once a string is no longer needed. Memory lost in this way—called a memory leak—accumulates over time, gradually crippling or even crashing a program. This will eventually require the program or computer system to be restarted.

In this laboratory, you develop a Text ADT that addresses these problems. The Text ADT specification that follows includes a diverse set of operations for manipulating strings.

The first decision you must make when implementing the Text ADT is how to store the characters in a string. Earlier, you saw that original C++ represented a string as a null-terminated sequence of characters in a one-dimensional buffer. Adopting this representation scheme allows you to reuse existing C++ functions in your implementation of the Text ADT. This code reuse, in turn, greatly simplifies the implementation process.

Your Text ADT will be more flexible if you dynamically allocate the memory used by the string buffer. The initial memory allocation for a buffer is done by a constructor. One of the constructors is invoked whenever a text declaration is encountered during the execution of a program. Which one is invoked depends on whether the declaration has as its argument an integer or a string literal. Once called, the constructor allocates a string buffer using C++'s `new[]` operator. The constructor that follows, for example, allocates a string buffer of `bufferSize` characters and assigns the address of the string buffer to the pointer `buffer`, where `buffer` is of type `char*`.

```
Text:: Text ( char* chaseSeq = "" )
{
    ...
    buffer = new char [bufferSize];
}
```

Whenever you allocate memory, you must ensure that it is deallocated when it is no longer needed. The class destructor is used to deallocate a string buffer. This function is invoked whenever a string variable goes out of scope—that is, whenever the function containing the corresponding variable declaration terminates. The fact that the call to the destructor is made automatically eliminates the possibility of you forgetting to deallocate the buffer. The following destructor frees the memory used by the string buffer allocated previously.

```
Text:: ~Text ()
{
    ...
    delete [] buffer;
}
```

Constructors and destructors are not the only operations that allocate and deallocate memory. The assignment operation may also need to perform memory allocation/ deallocation in order to extend the length of a string buffer to accommodate additional characters.

Strings can be of various lengths and the length of a given string can change as a result of an assignment. Your string representation should account for these variations in length by storing the length of the string (bufferSize) along with a pointer to the buffer containing the characters in the string (buffer). The resulting string representation is described by the following declarations.

```
int bufferSize;    // Size of the text buffer
char *buffer;      // Text buffer containing a null-terminated
                   // sequence of characters
```

Defaulting parameters: C++ allows the programmer to set up default values for parameters to a function. A default parameter is used in the Text constructor function. Given the function prototype

```
Text ( const char* charSeq = "" );
```

the constructor function should be called with some sort of C-string as a parameter. E.g., a new Text object could be declared by writing

```
Text myText("This is my text");
```

in which case the constructor parameter charSeq points to the C-string "This is my text". However, if the programmer instead creates a new Text object by writing

```
Text myText2();
```

then the compiler will make charSeq point to the empty C-string "".

Self-assignment protection: C++ allows the programmer to overload the assignment operator. For example, the following function will set the value of the Text object to the contents of other. We have to deal with the situation when other refers to the object to be changed (self-assignment). The "this != &other" code performs the self-assignment check. See the Laboratory 5 implementation notes pointer section for a more detailed explanation of what this code does.

```
void Text:: operator= ( const Text& other ) {
    if (this != &other) {
        . . .
    }
}
```

Double inclusion protection: C++ allows source code files to include other source code files by using the C++ preprocessor #include "filename" syntax. This is commonly done to include class and library declaration header files. The problem is that as files include one or more other files, which may in turn include others, it is quite easy to #include the same file more than once. Then the compiler issues errors about double declarations. The standard way to avoid this problem is to use the C++ preprocessor label definition mechanism to ensure that code only gets processed once. To avoid double-including the *Text.h* file, the file is written so as to define a preprocessor variable based on the name of the file. We take the file name, change the '.' to a '_' (because periods are not legal in the preprocessor names), and structure the file as follows:

```
#ifndef TEXT_H
#define TEXT_H
...              // Rest of code in file
#endif
```

When the compiler preprocessor is reading the file, it encounters the `#ifndef TEXT_H` statement. "ifndef" means "IF Not DEFined". The string `#ifndef TEXT_H` asks whether the preprocessor has created (defined) an identifier called `TEXT_H`. If a TEXT_H identifier has not been created, the statement is true; it processes the `#define TEXT_H` statement, defines a `TEXT_H` identifier, and processes everything else in the file up through the `#endif` statement. Next time the file gets included, TEXT_H is already defined, so the #ifndef TEXT_H is false and all lines get skipped through the #endif.

Step 1: Implement the operations in the Text ADT using this string representation scheme. Base your implementation on the following class declaration from the file *Text.h*.

(Note: all header files for this book are included in the student file set. We are including a copy of the header file for this lab for the student's convenience while being introduced to implementing ADTs with C++.)

```
class Text
{
  public:
    // Constructors and operator=
    Text ( const char* charSeq = "" );        // Initialize using char*
    Text ( const Text& other );               // Copy constructor
    void operator = ( const Text& other );    // Assignment
    // Destructor
    ~Text ();
    // Text operations
    int getLength () const;                          // # characters
    char operator [] ( int n ) const;               // Subscript
    void clear ();                                   // Clear string
    // Output the string structure -- used in testing/debugging
    void showStructure () const;
    // toUpper/toLower operations (Exercise 2)
    Text toUpper( ) const;                      // Create lower-case copy
    Text toLower( ) const;                      // Create upper-case copy
    // Relational operations (Exercise 3)
    bool operator == ( const Text& other ) const;
    bool operator <  ( const Text& other ) const;
    bool operator >  ( const Text& other ) const;
  private:
    // Data members
    int bufferSize;   // Size of the string buffer
    char* buffer;     // Text buffer containing a null-terminated char
                      //   sequence
};
```

Step 2: Save your implementation of the Text ADT in the file *Text.cpp*. Be sure to document your code.

Compilation Directions

Compile your implementation of the Text ADT in the file *Text.cpp* and the test program in the file *test1.cpp*. Compilation directions will depend on your compiler and operating system. This will typically be through a project file or through the command line.

Testing

Test your implementation of the Text ADT using the program in the file *test1.cpp*.

Step 1: Download the online test plans for Lab 1.

Lab 1 Online Test Plans

Test	Action
1-1	Tests the constructors.
1-2	Tests the length operation.
1-3	Tests the subscript operation.
1-4	Tests the assignment and clear operations.

Step 2: Complete the test plan for Test 1-1 by filling in the expected result for each string.

Step 3: Execute Test Plan 1-1. If you discover mistakes in your implementation of the Text ADT, correct them and execute the test plan again.

Step 4: Complete the test plan for Test 1-2 by filling in the length of each Text object.

Step 5: Execute the test plan. If you discover mistakes in your implementation of the Text ADT, correct them and execute the test plan again.

Step 6: Complete the test plan for Test 1-3 by filling in the character returned by the subscript operation for each value of n and the string "alpha". Remember, the description of the subscript operator ('[]') states that given [n], it returns the nth character, counting from zero. Otherwise, it returns char('\0').

Step 7: Execute the test plan. If you discover mistakes in your implementation of the Text ADT, correct them and execute the test plan again.

Step 8: Complete the test plan for Test 1-4 by filling in the expected result for each assignment statement.

Step 9: Execute the test plan. If you discover mistakes in your implementation of the Text ADT, correct them and execute the test plan again.

Programming Exercise 1

A compiler begins the compilation process by dividing a program into a set of delimited strings called tokens. This task is referred to as lexical analysis. For instance, given the C++ statement,

```
if ( j <= 10 ) cout << endl ;
```

lexical analysis by a C++ compiler produces the following ten tokens.

```
"if"  "("  "j"  "<="  "10"  ")"  "cout"  "<<"  "endl"  ";"
```

Before you can perform lexical analysis, you need operations that support the input and output of delimited strings. A pair of Text ADT input/output operations is described here.

```
friend istream& operator >> ( istream& input,
                              Text& inputText )
```

Requirements:
The specified input stream must not be in an error state.

Returns:
Extracts (inputs) a string from the specified input stream, returns it in `inputText`, and returns the resulting state of the input stream. It begins the input process by reading whitespace (blanks, newlines, and tabs) until a non-whitespace character is encountered. This non-whitespace character is returned as the first character in the string. It continues reading the Text string character-by-character until another whitespace character is encountered.

```
friend ostream& operator << ( ostream& output,
                              const Text& outputText )
```

Requirements:
The specified output stream must not be in an error state.

Returns:
Inserts (outputs) `outputText` in the specified output stream and returns the resulting state of the output stream.
    Note that these operations are *not* part of the Text class. However, they do need to have access to the data members of this class. Thus, they are named as friends of the Text class.

Step 1:   The file *textio.cpp* contains implementations of these Text string input/output operations. Copy these operations into your implementation of the Text ADT in the file *Text.cpp*. Prototypes for these operations are included in the declaration of Text class in the file *Text.h*.

Step 2:   Create a program that uses the operations in the Text ADT to perform lexical analysis on a text file containing a C++ program. Save your program in the file *lexical.cpp*. Your program should read the tokens in this file and output each token to the screen using the following format.

```
1 : [1stToken]
2 : [2ndToken]
...
```

This format requires that your program maintain a running count of the number of tokens that have been read from the text file. Assume that the tokens in the text file are delimited by whitespace—an assumption that is not true for C++ programs in general.

Step 3: Test your lexical analysis program using the C++ program in the file *progsamp.dat* as input. The contents of this file are shown here.

```
void main ( )
{
    int j ,
        total = 0 ;
    for ( j = 1 ; j <= 20 ; j ++ )
        total += j ;
}
```

Test your program using Test Plan 1-5.

Programming Exercise 2

It is useful to have a way of getting an entirely uppercase or entirely lowercase copy of a string. For this exercise, you are to implement the Text class `toUpper` and `toLower` member functions that return uppercase and lowercase copies of the Text object.

`Text toUpper( ) const`

Requirements:
None

Results:
Returns a new Text object containing an entirely uppercase copy of the object's internal text string.

`Text toLower( ) const`

Requirements:
None

Results:
Returns a new Text object containing an entirely lowercase copy of the object's internal text string.

Implementing each function requires creating a new object that is initialized with a C-string composed of the characters in the Text object, where all alphabetic characters are of the correct upper or lower case. The C++ `toupper` and `tolower` library functions are helpful in doing the case conversion. For instance, given a character `ch`, `toupper(ch)` returns the uppercase value of `ch` if `ch` is alphabetic. Otherwise it returns the unaltered value of `ch`. When using these functions, use "`#include <cctype>`".

Step 1: Implement the operations described above and add them to the file *Text.cpp*. Prototypes for these operations are included in the declaration of the Text class in the file *Text.h*.

Step 2: Activate Test 1 in the test program *test1.cpp* by changing the definition of LAB1_TEST1 from 0 to 1 in *config.h* and recompiling.

Step 3: Complete the test plan for Test 1-6 by filling in the expected result for each test.

Step 4: Execute Test Plan 1-6. If you discover mistakes in your implementation of the copy constructor, correct them and execute the test plan again.

Programming Exercise 3

Most applications that use strings will at some point sort the string data into alphabetical order, either to make their output easier to read or to improve program performance. In order to sort strings, you first must develop relational operations that compare the Text strings with one another.

```
bool operator == ( const Text& other )
```

Requirements:
None

Results:
Returns `true` if the object is lexically equivalent to `other`. Otherwise, returns `false`.

```
bool operator < ( const Text& other )
```

Requirements:
None

Results:
Returns `true` if the object occurs lexically before `other`. Otherwise, returns `false`.

```
bool operator > ( const Text& other )
```

Requirements:
None

Results:
Returns `true` if the object occurs lexically after `other`. Otherwise, returns `false`.

All of these operations require moving through a pair of Text object strings in parallel from beginning to end, comparing characters until a difference (if any) is found between the strings.

The standard C++ string library includes a function `strcmp` that can be used to compare C-strings character-by-character. You will need to "`#include <cstring>`" if you choose to use `strcmp`. Alternatively, you can develop your own code (or private member function) to perform this task.

Step 1: Implement the relational operations described above using the C++ `strcmp` function (or your own private member function) as a foundation. Add your implementation of these operations to the file *Text.cpp*. Prototypes for these operations are included in the declaration of the Text class in the file *Text.h*.

Step 2: Activate Test 2 in the test program *test1.cpp* by changing the definition of LAB1_TEST2 from 0 to 1 in *config.h* and recompiling.

Step 3: Complete the test plan for Test 1-7 by filling in the expected result for each pair of Text objects.

Step 4: Execute the test plan. If you discover mistakes in your implementation of the relational operations, correct them and execute the test plan again.

Analysis Exercise 1

A full-page version of this exercise with space for writing in answers is available in the online supplements for Lab 1.

Part A

What are the implications of having no destructor in a class like Text that does dynamic memory allocation? What are the practical consequences of not having a destructor for these classes in a long-running program?

Part B

What other operators might it make sense to overload in the Text class? Name four and briefly describe how they would work.

Part C

Are there any operators that it does not make sense to overload in the Text class? Why not?

Analysis Exercise 2

A full-page version of this exercise with space for writing in answers is available in the online supplements for Lab 1.

Part A

Design another method for the Text ADT and give its specification below. You need not implement the method, simply describe it.

Function prototype:

Requirements:

Results:

Part B

Describe an application in which you might use your new method.

BlogEntry ADT

In this laboratory, you

- gain additional experience implementing ADTs in C++.

- use previously defined C++ classes via composition.

- are introduced to the C++ exception mechanism.

- learn how to perform C++ member initialization.

- learn how to use static class methods.

ADT Overview

You probably know what a blog is, but in case your professor doesn't, we are going to briefly describe a blog. A blog is like an online diary where an author periodically posts short entries. The entries are typically arranged in reverse chronological order so that you can read the newest entries first and read your way backward toward the oldest entries.

The BlogEntry ADT encapsulates a single blog entry. It contains author, textual contents, and entry creation and modification dates. Since we conveniently have an implemented Text ADT, we will use it to represent the author and contents of the entry. The process of including one class within another is a form of code reuse called composition. To eliminate internal redundancy, we will develop a third ADT for the date information; we will also use the Date ADT through composition.

A common pattern for accessing data members in objects is to use member functions to set and get data values. These are commonly called getters and setters based on their functionality. We are following the common naming convention of using the prefixes set and get in the setter/getter function names, e.g., getAuthor. Not all data members require both a setter and a getter. For instance, the BlogEntry ADT only provides a getter for the dates. We do this because we want to enforce date integrity for these members by only allowing the ADT to modify them internally.

C++ Concepts Overview

We introduce the following new C++ concepts in this lab.

Member initialization: Including other objects in a class introduces an initialization problem. The default constructors for those objects will run automatically when the containing object's constructor runs. For instance, if a BlogEntry object is created, the default constructors for the Text and Date classes will automatically run. However, some objects may not have a default constructor, or the default constructor may not be the appropriate constructor in that case. Member initialization allows the programmer to specify which constructor to use. For consistency, C++ allows the programmer to use member initialization on the built-in data types, as well.

Exceptions: The standard C++ method for dealing with bad parameters and other difficult—or impossible—situations is to throw an exception. Throwing an exception causes the currently active function to stop execution and return to the calling function. Unless that function or one of its callers takes special steps to handle the exception, the program will be halted. The code that called the function can decide what to do when an exception is thrown. Common responses to an exception include one or more of the following: 1) print out a helpful explanation of what went wrong, 2) try to work around the problem, and 3) halt the program.

Static methods: It would sometimes be useful to call a class member function without requiring an instance of that class to exist. For example, the Date ADT provides a static method, isLeapYear, that determines whether a year is a leap year. We don't want to create a complete date object with a fictional day and month in order to determine whether the year is a leap year. Static methods can be invoked in the absence of a class instance.

Friends: The protection mechanisms of C++ are too coarse grained. We occasionally need to provide full access to our ADT to a limited set of external functions. By making those functions friends of our ADT, they can access the ADT's internal data structures. For all non-friends, the standard protection mechanisms hold. The most common use of friends is 1) to extend IOStream functionality to new ADTs, and 2) to develop highly coupled classes that may need access to each other's internal data. In this lab book, we use friends only to extend IOStream functionality.

BlogEntry ADT Specification

Data items

The author, the entry contents, and the creation and modification dates.

Structure

The structure is via composition of the Text and Date ADTs.

Operations

```
BlogEntry ( )
```

Requirements:
None

Results:
Default constructor. Creates an entry with unnamed author and empty contents. Uses the default constructors for all data items.

```
BlogEntry ( const Text& initAuthor, const Text& initContents )
```

Requirements:
None

Results:
Constructor. Creates an entry initialized to the specified author and contents. Uses the default constructors for both Date objects.

```
Text getAuthor ( ) const
```

Requirements:
None

Results:
Getter for author. Returns value of `author` object.

```
Text getContents ( ) const
```

Requirements:
None

Results:
Getter for contents. Returns value of `contents` object.

```
Date getCreateDate ( ) const
```

Requirements:
None

Results:
Getter for creation date. Returns value of `created` object.

```
Date getModifyDate ( ) const
```

Requirements:
None

Results:
Getter for modification date. Returns value of `modified` object.

```
void setAuthor ( const Text& newAuthor )
```

Requirements:
None

Results:
Setter for author. Sets value of `author` object.

```
void setContents ( const Text& newContents )
```

Requirements:
None

Results:
Setter for contents. Sets value of `contents` object.

```
void showStructure ( ) const
```

Requirements:
None

Results:
Outputs the contents of the BlogEntry. Note that this operation is intended for testing/debugging purposes only.

Date ADT Specification

Data items

A day, month, and year. All data values for these will start counting at 1, as is normal for dates.

Structure

All members are integer values.

Operations

`Date ( )`

Requirements:
None

Results:
Default constructor. Creates a date that represents the current date.

`Date ( int day, int month, int year ) throw ( logic_error )`

Requirements:
Parameters must represent a valid date.

Results:
Constructor. Creates a date that represents the specified date.

`int getDay ( ) const`

Requirements:
None

Results:
Getter for day of month. Returns the value of day.

`int getMonth ( ) const`

Requirements:
None

Results:
Getter for month. Returns the value of month.

`int getYear ( ) const`

Requirements:
None

Results:
Getter for year. Returns the value of year.

```
static bool isLeapYear( int year )
```

Requirements:
Year is greater than 1901 A.D.

Results:
Static method. If the specified year is a leap year, returns `true`. Else returns `false`.

```
static int daysInMonth ( int month, int year )
```

Requirements:
Year is greater than 1901 A.D. (The formula we provide uses 1901 as a basis for calculation.)

Results:
Static method. Returns the number of days in the specified month.

```
friend ostream& operator<< ( ostream& out, const Date& date )
```

Requirements:
None

Results:
Outputs the date in the same format as the showStructure function to the appropriate `ostream`. Note: Technically, this is not part of the Date ADT specification, but it is closely tied because it is a friend.

```
void showStructure () const
```

Requirements:
None

Results:
Outputs the day, month and year. Note that this operation is intended for testing/debugging purposes only.

Implementation Notes

Member initialization: This is performed in the constructor definition (implementation) after the parameter and exception lists, but before the constructor body's opening brace. The syntax is to begin with a colon (':'), followed by a comma-separated list of initialization elements. Each object initialization element is actually a call to a constructor for a specific member variable. Therefore, the syntax of an initialization element looks like a call to a constructor for that member variable. For example, here is an implementation for the BlogEntry ADT two-parameter constructor.

```
BlogEntry::BlogEntry(const Text& initAuthor,
                     const Text& initContents)
    : author(initAuthor), contents(initContents)

{
    // No additional code necessary
}
```

This code calls the Text constructor for the `author` object with `initAuthor` as a parameter. It then calls the Text constructor for the `contents` object with `initContents` as a parameter. Since no constructor is explicitly listed for the Date objects in the member initialization list, the Date object default constructors will be used. This covers all the BlogEntry member data, so no additional work needs to be done inside the BlogEntry constructor body.

Exceptions: The C++ exception handling mechanism is quite complicated. For the purposes of this book, 1) you will always be throwing a `logic_error` exception, and 2) we only discuss how to generate exceptions—not how to handle them after they are thrown.

Following are the steps for using exceptions in your data structure.

1. Include <stdexcept> in your C++ program file. We already included this in the header files.
2. When the function requirements (also known as prerequisites) are violated, throw an exception. The generic syntax is

   ```
   if ( condition ) throw logic_error("explanation string");
   ```

   The code in the program that deals with the exception can access the string and use it to improve error messages and interaction with the user.

   For instance, in the Date constructor, you can deal with an invalid month by writing

   ```
   if ( month < 1 || month > 12 )
       throw logic_error("month not in valid range");
   ```

3. The last step is to declare that the function throws an exception and which exceptions it may throw. This should be done in both the class declaration file—e.g., *Date.h*—and in the class definition file—e.g., *Date.cpp*. After the function parameter parentheses, write "`throw (logic_error)`". The syntax is the same for both cases.

Static methods: A class member function is made static by placing the keyword `static` in the function declaration. Note: there are many uses of the keyword `static` in C++. Do not use `static` in the function definition because it means something completely different. The syntax for using a static method is to use the class name, followed by the scope resolution operator ("::"), followed by the function name. E.g., "`if( Date::isLeapYear(2000) ) {...}`".

Friends: To make a function a friend of a particular class, use the keyword `friend` in the class declaration, followed by the friend function prototype. Then use the named function as normal; it will have full access to anything in the class, as though it were a class member function. For instance,

```
friend ostream& operator<<(ostream& out, const Date& date);
```

Composition detail: Typically, each class has its own declaration file (the ".h" file). When using composition in a class, you need to #include the class declaration files for each of the classes used in composition. This gives the compiler enough information to process the code correctly.

Extending iostream functionality: The iostream class cannot possibly know about all the new classes that you write. By default, it only knows how to deal with the built-in data types. We often would like to use that same functionality with classes. This is accomplished by overloading the << and >> operators. These operators take two parameters: 1) a stream object, and 2) an object of the relevant class. To support compact input and output, (e.g., "cout << obj1 << obj2;", instead of two separate statements) the iostream class returns a reference to the stream object in these overloaded operators. To overload the << operator, use code similar to the following example for the Date implementation.

```
ostream& operator<<( ostream& out, const Date& date ) {
    return out << date.month << "/" << date.day << "/" << date.year;
}
```

The key to extending the iostream functionally successfully is 1) using a stream reference for both return type and stream parameter, 2) passing the proper values to the stream, and 3) returning the updated stream.

Step 1: Implement the operations in the two ADTs. Base your implementation on the declarations for the two classes as provided in *Date.h* and *BlogEntry.h*. The standard C++ library functions `time` and `localtime` can be used to access the necessary time and date information. You may need help from your instructor to get this working.

(Note: all header files for this book are included in the student file set. We included a copy of the header file in the first lab in this book for your convenience while getting introduced to implementing ADTs with C++. Throughout the rest of this lab text, please view the header files in the lab files distribution.)

Step 2: Save your implementation of the Date ADT in the file *Date.cpp*. Save your implementation of the BlogEntry ADT in the file *BlogEntry.cpp*. Be sure to document your code.

Compilation Directions

Compile your implementation of the Date ADT in the file *Date.cpp*, your implementation of the BlogEntry ADT in the file *BlogEntry.cpp*, and the test program in the file *test2.cpp*. Compilation details will depend on your programming environment.

Testing

Test your implementation of the Date and BlogEntry ADTs by using the program in the file *test2.cpp*.

Step 1: Download the online test plans for Lab 2.

Step 2: Complete the Test Plan for Test 2-1 by filling in the expected result for each date.

Step 3: Execute Test Plan 2-1. If you discover mistakes in your implementation of the Date ADT, correct them and execute the test plan again.

Step 4: Complete the test plan for Test 2-2 by filling in the expected result for each getter.

Step 5: Execute Test Plan 2-2. If you discover mistakes in your implementation of the Date ADT, correct them and execute the test plan again.

Step 6: Complete the test plan for Test 2-3 by filling in the expected result for each leap year.

Step 7: Execute Test Plan 2-3. If you discover mistakes in your implementation of the Date ADT, correct them and execute the test plan again.

Step 8: Complete the test plan for Test 2-4 by filling in the expected result for each month.

Step 9: Execute Test Plan 2-4. If you discover mistakes in your implementation of the Date ADT, correct them and execute the test plan again.

Step 10: Complete the test plan for Test 2-5 by filling in the expected output for each date.

Step 11: Execute Test Plan 2-5. If you discover mistakes in your implementation of the Date ADT, correct them and execute the test plan again.

Step 12: Complete the test plan for Test 2-6 by filling in the expected result for each blog entry.

Step 13: Execute Test Plan 2-6. If you discover mistakes in your implementation of the BlogEntry ADT, correct them and execute the test plan again.

Step 14: Complete the test plan for Test 2-7 by filling in the expected result for each getter and setter.

Step 15: Execute Test Plan 2-7. If you discover mistakes in your implementation of the BlogEntry ADT, correct them and execute the test plan again.

Programming Exercise 1

The Web has become integral to computing. Many applications now use a web browser as the standard interface. Consequently, it is helpful to be able to generate output in HTML. It is also natural to generate HTML for web-based information delivery systems, such as blogs.

```
void printHTML ( ostream& out ) const
```

Requirements:
None

Results:
Sends output to the stream out in the format specified below.

Output Format Specification

```
<html>
<body>
<h1>author here</h1>
<p>
contents here
</p>
<p>
Created: creation date here
</p>
<p>
Last modified: modification date here
</p>
</body>
</html>
```

Note that the output web page is just begging for enhancement (e.g., Title, CSS styling, etc.). A lot of the extra information would belong in an expanded BlogEntry ADT.

Step 1:   Add this function to your implementation of the BlogEntry ADT.

Step 2:   Activate Test 8 in the test program *test2.cpp* by changing the definition of LAB2_TEST8 from 0 to 1 in *config.h* and recompiling.

Step 3:   Complete the test plan for Test 2-8 by filling in the expected result for each test.

Step 4:   Execute Test Plan 2-8. If you discover mistakes in your implementation of printHTML, correct them and execute the test plan again.

Programming Exercise 2

In order to produce a calendar for a given date, you need to know on which day of the week the date occurs. We are going to enhance the Date ADT to provide access to this information by adding the following member function.

```
int getDayOfWeek( ) const
```

Requirements:
None

Results:
Returns a value between 0 (Sunday) and 6 (Saturday) indicating the day of the week.

The day of the week corresponding to a date can be computed using the following formula:

$$dayOfWeek = (\ 1 + nYears + nLeapYears + nDaysToMonth + day\ )\ \%\ 7$$

where *nYears* is the number of years since 1901, *nLeapYears* is the number of leap years since 1901, and *nDaysToMonth* is the number of days from the start of the year to the start of `month`.

This formula yields a value between 0 (Sunday) and 6 (Saturday) and is accurate for any date from January 1, 1901 through at least December 31, 2099. You can compute the value *nDaysToMonth* dynamically using a loop. Alternatively, you can use an array to store the number of days before each month in a nonleap year and add a correction for leap years when needed.

Step 1: Add this function to your implementation of the Date ADT.

Step 2: Activate Test 9 in the test program *test2.cpp* by changing the definition of LAB2_TEST9 from 0 to 1 in *config.h* and recompiling.

Step 3: Complete the test plan for Test 2-9 by filling in the expected result for each test.

Step 4: Execute Test Plan 2-9. If you discover mistakes in your implementation of `getDayOfWeek`, correct them and execute the test plan again.

Programming Exercise 3

Most applications that use dates will at some point need to sort them in chronological order. It is much easier if the relational operators are overloaded to support date comparison.

```
bool operator== ( const Date& other ) const
```

Requirements:
None

Results:
Returns `true` if this object represents the same date as `other`. Otherwise, returns `false`.

```
bool operator< ( const Date& other ) const
```

Requirements:
None

Results:
Returns `true` if this object represents an earlier date than `other`. Otherwise, returns `false`.

```
bool operator> ( const Date& other ) const
```

Requirements:
None

Results:
Returns `true` if this object represents a later date than `other`. Otherwise, returns `false`.

Step 1: Implement the relational operations described above. Add your implementation of these operations to the file *Date.cpp*. Prototypes for these operations are included in the declaration of the Date class in the file *Date.h*.

Step 2: Activate Test 10 in the test program *test2.cpp* by changing the definition of LAB2_TEST10 from 0 to 1 in *config.h*.

Step 3: Complete the test plan for Test 2-10 by filling in the expected result for each test. Add your own test cases to Test Plan 2-10 so it is complete.

Step 4: Execute Test Plan 2-10. If you discover mistakes in your implementation of the relational operations, correct them and execute the test plan again.

Analysis Exercise 1

A full-page version of this exercise with space for writing in answers is available in the online supplements for Lab 2.

Part A

Design another operation for the BlogEntry ADT and give its specification below. You need not implement the operation, simply describe it.

Function prototype:

Requirements:

Results:

Part B

Describe an application in which you might use your new operation.

Analysis Exercise 2

A full-page version of this exercise with space for writing in answers is available in the online supplements for Lab 2.

The BlogEntry class name suggests that it would be used by composition in a Blog class. Design the Blog ADT, specifying data items, structure, and operations. For each operation, indicate the prototype, any requirements, and the results.

Data Items

Structure

Operations

We provide one example operation to indicate the format and level of detail expected.

```
BlogEntry& operator[]( int entryNumber ) throw ( logic_error )
```

Requirements:
entryNumber must represent a valid entry.

Results:
Returns a reference to the specified blog entry.

Array Implementation of the List ADT

In this laboratory you

- implement the List ADT using an array representation of a list.

- develop an iteration scheme that allows you to move through a list data item-by-data item.

- learn how to use C++ templates to create generic data types.

- are exposed to implementing base classes in an inheritance hierarchy.

- analyze the algorithmic complexity of your array implementation of the List ADT.

Objectives

ADT Overview

If an ADT is to be useful, its operations must be both expressive and intuitive. The List ADT described below provides operations that allow you to insert data items in a list, remove data items from a list, check the state of a list (Is it empty? or Is it full?), and iterate through the data items in a list. Iteration is done using a cursor that you move through the list much as you move the cursor in a text editor or word processor. Iteration functions typically allow the cursor to be moved to the beginning, the end, the next, or the prior item in a data structure. In the following example, the List ADT's gotoBeginning operation is used to move the cursor to the beginning of the list. The cursor is then moved through the list data item-by-data item by repeated applications of the gotoNext operation. Note that the data item marked by the cursor is shown in bold italics.

After gotoBeginning: *a*   b   c   d
After gotoNext: a   *b*   c   d
After gotoNext: a   b   *c*   d
After gotoNext: a   b   c   *d*

C++ Concepts Overview

Templates: C++ supports the concept of a generic data type through templates. Generic data types allow a class to be implemented in a generic way such that one or more data types in the class do not need to be specified when the class is implemented. The code is written independent of the data type that will eventually be specified when objects of the class are instantiated.

Although all programs share the same definition of list—a sequence of homogeneous data items—the type of data item stored in lists varies from program to program. Some use lists of integers, others use lists of characters, floating-point numbers, points, and so forth. You normally have to decide on the data item's type at the time that you implement the ADT. If you need a different data item type, there are several possibilities.

1. You could edit the class code (e.g., the declaration file, *classname.h*, and the definition file, *classname.cpp*—in the case of this List ADT, *ListArray.h* and *ListArray.cpp*) and replace every reference to the old data type by the new data type. This is a lot of work, tedious, and error prone.
2. A simpler solution is to use a made up data type name throughout the class—e.g., `DataType`—and then use the C++ `typedef` statement at the beginning of the class declaration file to specify what `DataType` really is. To specify that the list data items should be characters, you would type

```
typedef DataType char;
```

This approach does work and changing the data item data type is much easier than the first solution; you just change the `typedef` line and recompile.

It does however, have problems. For instance, a given program can only have `DataType` set to one particular type. You cannot have both a list of characters and a list of integers in the same program; `DataType` must be either `char` or `int`. You could make entire copies of the List ADT and define a new `DataType` differently in each copy. Because you cannot have multiple classes in a program with exactly the same name, you must also change every occurrence of the class name `List` to something like `CharList` or `IntList`. This will work, but it takes you back to solution #1 and is generally unsatisfactory.

3. Fortunately, C++ has a solution: templates. Using templates, you do not need to create a different list implementation for each type of data item. Instead, you create a list implementation in terms of list data items of some generic type rather like solution two above. This requires just one copy of the class implementation source code. You can then ask the compiler to make any number of lists whose data items are an arbitrary data type by adding a simple piece of information—the data type inside angle brackets, e.g. `List<float>`—when you declare a list in your code. For instance, to create a list of integers and one of characters in the same program, you would write the following:

```
List<int> samples;      // Create a list of integers
List<char> line;        // Then create a list of characters
```

Inheritance: In Lab 4, we are going to introduce the concept of inheritance. Lab 3 is the foundation on which Lab 4 will be based. The primary requirements are declaring some class members protected instead of private, and declaring functions `virtual`.

Virtual functions: By declaring a function `virtual`, we are stating that it may be overridden in another class that is connected to this class through inheritance.

List ADT Specification

Data Items

The data items in a list are of generic type DataType.

Structure

The data items form a linear structure in which list data items follow one after the other, from the beginning of the list to its end. The ordering of the data items is determined by when and where each data item is inserted into the list and is *not* a function of the data contained in the list data items. At any point in time, one data item in any nonempty list is marked using the list's cursor. You travel through the list using operations that change the position of the cursor.

Operations

`List ( int maxNumber = MAX_LIST_SIZE )`

Requirements:
None

Results:
Constructor. Creates an empty list. Allocates enough memory for the list containing `maxNumber` data items.

```
List ( const List& other )
```

Requirements:
None

Results:
Copy constructor. Initializes the list to be equivalent to the `other` List object parameter.

```
List& operator= ( const List& other )
```

Requirements:
None

Results:
Overloaded assignment operator. Sets the list to be equivalent to the `other` object parameter and returns a reference to the object.

```
virtual ~List ()
```

Requirements:
None

Results:
Destructor. Deallocates (frees) the memory used to store the list.

```
virtual void insert ( const DataType& newDataItem )
               throw ( logic_error )
```

Requirements:
List is not full.

Results:
Inserts `newDataItem` into the list. If the list is not empty, then inserts `newDataItem` after the cursor. Otherwise, inserts `newDataItem` as the first (and only) data item in the list. In either case, moves the cursor to `newDataItem`.

```
void remove () throw ( logic_error )
```

Requirements:
List is not empty.

Results:
Removes the data item marked by the cursor from the list. If the resulting list is not empty, the cursor should now be marking the data item that followed the deleted data item. If the deleted data item was at the end of the list, then the cursor marks the data item at the beginning of the list. This operation preserves the order of the remaining data items in the list.

```
virtual void replace ( const DataType& newDataItem )
                throw ( logic_error )
```

Requirements:
List is not empty.

Results:
Replaces the data item marked by the cursor with `newDataItem`. The cursor remains at `newDataItem`.

```
void clear ()
```

Requirements:
None

Results:
Removes all the data items in the list.

```
bool isEmpty () const
```

Requirements:
None

Results:
Returns `true` if the list is empty. Otherwise, returns `false`.

```
bool isFull () const
```

Requirements:
None

Results:
Returns `true` if the list is full. Otherwise, returns `false`.

```
void gotoBeginning () throw ( logic_error )
```

Requirements:
List is not empty.

Results:
If the list is not empty, then moves the cursor to the data item at the beginning of the list.

```
void gotoEnd () throw ( logic_error )
```

Requirements:
List is not empty.

Results:
If the list is not empty, then moves the cursor to the data item at the end of the list.

```
bool gotoNext () throw ( logic_error )
```

Requirements:

List is not empty.

Results:

If the cursor is not at the end of the list, then moves the cursor to the next data item in the list and returns `true`. Otherwise, returns `false`.

```
bool gotoPrior () throw ( logic_error )
```

Requirements:

List is not empty.

Results:

If the cursor is not at the beginning of the list, then moves the cursor to the preceding data item in the list and returns `true`. Otherwise, returns `false`.

```
DataType getCursor () const throw ( logic_error )
```

Requirements:

List is not empty.

Results:

Returns the value of the data item marked by the cursor.

```
void showStructure () const
```

Requirements:
None

Results:

Outputs the data items in the list. If the list is empty, outputs "Empty list". Note that this operation is intended for testing/debugging purposes only. It only supports list data items that are one of C++'s predefined data types (`int`, `char`, and so forth) or that have had the << operator overloaded for an `ostream`.

Implementation Notes

Templates: A template is something that serves as a pattern. The pattern is not the final product, but is used to enable faster production of a final product. Every place in your code where you would normally have to specify the data type, you instead use an arbitrary string to represent any actual data type that you might later wish to use. We will use the arbitrary string `"DataType"` to represent the generic data type. Nowhere does either the class declaration—the *class.h* file—or the class definition—the *class.cpp* file—specify the actual C++ data type. You can defer specifying the actual data type until it is time to instantiate—create—an object of that class.

Following are a few simple rules for creating and using a template class.

- The string "`template < typename DataType >`" must go right before the class declaration and before every class member function definiton. Remember, `DataType` is our arbitrary identifier that will represent any data type in the template class. So the lines

```
class List
{
  public:
    ...
```

are changed to

```
template < typename DataType >
class List
{
  public:
    ...
```

The start of a function definition that used to be

```
List:: List ( int maxNumber )
```

now becomes

```
template < typename DataType >
List<DataType>:: List ( int maxNumber )
```

- Every use of the class name now must include the generic data type name enclosed in angle brackets. Every instance of the string "`List`" becomes "`List<DataTtype>`". In the example constructor definition, the class resolution "`List::`" becomes "`List<DataType>::`". Also note that the exception to the rule is that the constructor name is not modified—it remains just "`List`".

```
template < typename DataType >
List<DataType>:: List ( int maxNumber )
```

- When it is time to instantiate an object of that class, the real data type—inside angle brackets—is appended to the class name. So the following lines create a list of 10 integers and a list of 80 characters

```
// We tell the compiler to make a copy of the generic list just
// for integers and to make another just for characters.
List<int>  samples(10);
List<char> line(80);
```

Note: C++ originally used the syntax "`<class DataType>`" before templated classes and functions. The use of "class" was confusing to programmers since DataType could be a built-in type. The syntax was eventually changed to be "`<typename DataType>`". C++ continues to permit the use of "class" in this context, but "typename" is preferred.

Class constants: We have a fairly strong opinion about declaring class constants (and reasons for our preference). We prefer to declare class constants inside the class—as opposed to somewhere outside the class declaration—and to make them "static" variables. Because they are part of the class, declaring them inside the class associates them more closely with a class. This also allows programmers to reference the constants from anywhere by using the `ClassName::CONST_NAME` syntax (assuming the class protection policy allows access), without having to first create an object of that class. Declaring it to be `static` also allows initialization of the constant within the class, something otherwise illegal. Last, declaring a variable or constant identifier as `static` guarantees that all objects of that class will share the same variable or constant, thus reducing program memory requirements.

```
class X {
    ...
    static const int MY_MAX = 10;
    ...
};
```

Exceptions: The use of exceptions is explained in Lab 2. If you skipped Lab 2, please go back and read the explanations in the "C++ Concepts" and "Implementation Notes" sections.

Writing classes for inheritance: Inheritance is one of the significant characteristics of object-oriented programming. Given a class—let's call it Base—we can write another class—call it Derived—that can be derived from the base class by inheriting data and member functions from the class. The important thing to be aware of when developing a base class is that anything in its private section is truly private, even from a derived class. The solution is to put anything that is to be kept private from code outside the inheritance hierarchy, but that must be accessible to derived classes, in a *protected* section. The syntax is similar to how a private section is declared, only the word "protected" is substituted for "private". Whether a base class will also have a private section depends on whether there are operations or data values that must be kept private even from derived classes.

You can implement a list in many ways. Given that all the data items in a list are of the same type, and that the list structure is linear, an array seems a natural choice.

Step 1: Implement the operations in the List ADT using an array to store the list data items. Lists change in size, therefore you need to store the maximum number of data items the list can hold (`maxSize`) and the actual number of data items in the list (`size`), along with the list data items themselves (`dataItems`). You also need to keep track of the cursor array index (`cursor`). Base your implementation on the declarations from the file *ListArray.h*. An implementation of the `showStructure` operation is given in the file *show3.cpp*. Please insert the contents of *show3.cpp* into your *ListArray.cpp* file.

Step 2: Save your implementation of the List ADT in the file *ListArray.cpp*. Be sure to document your code.

Compilation Directions

Compiling programs that use templated classes requires a change in what files are included using the #include preprocessor directive, and in how the program is compiled. Because of how C++ compilers process templated code, the program that creates objects of the classes (e.g., *test3.cpp*) must include the class implementation file, not the class declaration file. That is, it must do #include "ClassName.cpp" instead of the usual #include "ClassName.h". The rule is in effect for the rest of this book. Because the main implementation file does a #include of the class implementation code, the class implementation code is not compiled separately.

Testing

The test programs that you used in Laboratories 1 and 2 consisted of a series of tests that were hardcoded into the programs. Adding a new test case to this style of test program requires changing the test program itself. In this and subsequent laboratories, you use a more flexible kind of test program to evaluate your ADT implementations, one in which you specify a test case using commands, rather than code. These interactive, command-driven test programs allow you to check a new test case by simply entering a series of keyboard commands and observing the results.

The test program in the file *test3.cpp*, for instance, supports the following commands.

Command	Action
+x	Insert data item x after the cursor.
–	Remove the data item marked by the cursor.
=x	Replace the data item marked by the cursor with data item x.
@	Display the data item marked by the cursor.
N	Go to the next data item.
P	Go to the prior data item.
<	Go to the beginning of the list.
>	Go to the end of the list.
E	Report whether the list is empty.
F	Report whether the list is full.
C	Clear the list.
Q	Quit the test program.

Suppose you wish to confirm that your array implementation of the List ADT successfully inserts a data item into a list that has been emptied by a series of calls to the remove operation. You can test this case by entering the following sequence of keyboard commands.

Command	+a	+b	–	–	+c	Q
Action	Insert a	Insert b	Remove	Remove	Insert c	Quit

It is easy to see how this interactive test program allows you to rapidly examine a variety of test cases. This speed comes with a price, however. You must be careful not to violate the preconditions required by the operations that you are testing. For instance, the commands

Command	+a	+b	–	–	–
Action	Insert a	Insert b	Remove	Remove	Causes Error

cause the test program to fail during the last call to the remove operation. The source of the failure does not lie in the implementation of the List ADT, nor is the test program flawed. The failure occurs because this sequence of operations creates a state that violates the preconditions of the remove operation (the list must *not* be empty when the remove operation is invoked). The speed with which you can create and evaluate test cases using an interactive, command-driven test program makes it very easy to produce this kind of error. It is very tempting to just sit down and start entering commands. A much better strategy, however, is to create a test plan listing the test cases you wish to check and then to write out command sequences that generate these test cases.

Step 1: Download the online test plans for Lab 3.

Step 2: Complete the Test Plan 3-1 by adding test cases that check whether your implementation of the List ADT correctly handles the following tasks:

- insertions into a newly emptied list
- insertions that fill a list to its maximum size
- deletions from a full list
- determining whether a list is empty
- determining whether a list is full

Assume that the output of one test case is used as the input to the following test case, and note that although expected results are listed for the final command in each command sequence, you should confirm that *each* command produces a correct result.

Step 3: Execute your test plan. If you discover mistakes in your implementation of the List ADT, correct them and execute your test plan again.

Step 4: Activate Test 1 by changing the value of LAB3_TEST1 from 0 to 1 in the *config.h* file. The second test changes the data type being used by the List from a character to an integer.

Step 5: Recompile the test program.

Step 6: Replace the character data in your test plan with integer values to create Test Plan 3-2.

Step 7: Execute your revised test plan using the revised test program. If you discover mistakes in your implementation of the List ADT, correct them and execute your revised test plan again.

Programming Exercise 1

The genetic information encoded in a strand of deoxyribonucleic acid (DNA) is stored in the purine and pyrimidine bases (adenine, guanine, cytosine, and thymine) that form the strand. Biologists are keenly interested in the bases in a DNA sequence because these bases determine what the sequence does.

By convention, DNA sequences are represented by using lists containing the letters 'A', 'G', 'C', and 'T' (for adenine, guanine, cytosine, and thymine, respectively). The following function computes one property of a DNA sequence—the number of times each base occurs in the sequence.

```
void countBases ( List& dnaSequence, int& aCount,
                  int& cCount, int& tCount, int& gCount )
```

Input parameters:
dnaSequence: contains the bases in a DNA sequence encoded using the characters
'A', 'C', 'T', and 'G'.

Output parameters:
aCount, cCount, tCount, gCount: the number of times the corresponding base appears in the DNA sequence.

Step 1: Copy the file *test3dna.cs* with the shell program to the file *test3dna.cpp*. Implement this function and add it to the program in the file *test3dna.cpp*. Your implementation should manipulate the DNA sequence using the operations in the List ADT.

Step 2: The program in the file *test3dna.cpp* reads a DNA sequence from the keyboard, calls the countBases function, and outputs the resulting base counts. Complete Test Plan 3-3 by adding DNA sequences of different lengths and various combinations of bases.

Step 3: Execute your test plan. If you discover mistakes in your implementation of the countBases function, correct them and execute your test plan again.

Programming Exercise 2

In many applications, the ordering of the data items in a list changes over time. Not only are new data items added and existing ones removed, but data items are repositioned within the list. The following List ADT operation moves a data item to a new position in a list.

```
void moveToNth ( int n ) throw ( logic_error )
```

Requirements:
List contains at least n+1 data items (because n=0 represents the first position).

Results:
Removes the data item marked by the cursor from the list and reinserts it as the *n*th data item in the list, where the data items are numbered from beginning to end, starting with zero. Moves the cursor to the moved data item.

Step 1: Implement this operation and add it to the file *ListArray.cpp*. A prototype for this operation is included in the declaration of the List class in the file *ListArray.h*.

Step 2: Activate Test 1 in the test program *test3.cpp* by changing the definition of LAB3_TEST1 from 0 to 1 in *config.h* and recompiling.

Step 3: Complete the Test Plan 3-4 by adding test cases that check whether your implementation of the moveToNth operation correctly processes moves within various sized lists.

Step 4: Execute Test Plan 3-4. If you discover mistakes in your implementation of the moveToNth operation, correct them and execute your test plan again.

Programming Exercise 3

Finding a particular list data item is another very common task. The following operation searches a list for a specified data item. The fact that the search begins with the data item marked by the cursor—and not the beginning of the list—means that this operation can be applied iteratively to locate all of the occurrences of a specified data item.

```
bool find ( const DataType& searchDataItem ) throw ( logic_error )
```

Requirements:
List is not empty.

Results:
Searches a list for `searchDataItem`. Begins the search with the data item marked by the cursor. Moves the cursor through the list until either `searchDataItem` is found (returns `true`) or the end of the list is reached without finding `searchDataItem` (returns `false`). Leaves the cursor at the last data item visited during the search.

Step 1: Implement this operation and add it to the file *ListArray.cpp*. A prototype for this operation is included in the declaration of the List class in the file *ListArray.h*.

Step 2: Activate Test 2 in the test program *test3.cpp* by changing the definition of LAB3_TEST2 from 0 to 1 in *config.h* and recompiling.

Step 3: Complete the Test Plan 3-5 by adding test cases that check whether your implementation of the find operation correctly conducts searches in full lists, as well as searches that begin with the last data item in a list.

Step 4: Execute the test plan. If you discover mistakes in your implementation of the find operation, correct them and execute your test plan again.

Analysis Exercise 1

A full-page version of these exercises with space for writing in answers is available in the online supplements for Lab 3.

Given a list containing N data items, develop worst-case, order-of-magnitude estimates of the execution time of the following List ADT operations, assuming they are implemented using an array. Briefly explain your reasoning behind each estimate.

```
gotoNext   O(      )

Explanation:
```

```
gotoPrior   O(      )

Explanation:
```

```
insert   O(      )

Explanation:
```

```
remove   O(      )

Explanation:
```

Analysis Exercise 2

Part A

Give a declaration for a list of floating-point numbers called `echoReadings`. Assume that the list can contain no more than fifty floating-point numbers.

Part B

Give the declarations required for a list of (x, y, z)-coordinates called `coords`. Assume that x, y, and z are floating-point numbers and that there will be no more than twenty coordinates in the list.

Part C

Are the declarations that you created in Parts A and B compatible with the operations in your implementation of the List ADT? Briefly explain why or why not.

Ordered List ADT

In this laboratory you

- implement the Ordered List ADT using an array to store the list data items and use a binary search to locate data items.

- use inheritance to derive a new class from an existing one.

- explore a number of issues that relate to programming with inheritance.

- analyze the efficiency of your implementation of the Ordered List ADT.

ADT Overview

In an ordered list the data items are maintained in ascending (or descending) order based on the data contained in the list data items. Typically, the contents of one field are used to determine the ordering. This field is referred to as the key field, or the key. In this laboratory, we assume that each data item in an ordered list has a key that uniquely identifies the data item—that is, no two data items in any ordered list have the same key. As a result, you can use a data item's key to efficiently retrieve the data item from a list.

There is a great deal of similarity between the Ordered List ADT and the List ADT. In fact, with the exception of the insert, retrieve, and replace operations, these ADTs are identical. Rather than implementing the Ordered List ADT from the ground up, you can take advantage of these similarities by using your array implementation of the List ADT from Laboratory 3 as a foundation for an array implementation of the Ordered List ADT.

C++ Concepts Overview

Inheritance: Inheritance is the major new topic in this lab. C++ supports the ability for a class to extend another class's functionality. This is done by having the new class (the derived class) inherit the traits of the existing class (the base class) and adding new traits to the derived class. All of the following concepts relate to inheritance.

Access control: As a reminder, access to data and member functions from outside the class is governed by declaring them in one of three sections of the class: public, private, and protected. Items in the `private` section are not accessible to derived classes. Member functions and data in the `protected` section are accessible to derived classes, but are protected from any other access.

Virtual functions: To indicate which functions the base class intends to allow a derived class to override, the keyword `virtual` is placed in each function's signature in the base class declaration. It is also standard to use virtual in the derived class in order to 1) provide documentation, and 2) allow the derived class to be used as a base class for a third class.

Base class constructors: When a constructor of a derived class is called, the default behavior of the C++ compiler is to call the default constructor for the base class. This will often produce incorrect results, so a mechanism is provided to specify which base class constructor to execute.

Virtual destructors: If a class is designed to serve as a base class, its destructor should be declared virtual to allow any derived class's destructor to function correctly.

Ordered List ADT

Data Items:

The data items in an ordered list are of generic type DataType. Each data item has a key of the generic type KeyType that uniquely identifies the data item. Data items usually include additional data. Type DataType must provide a function called `getKey` that returns a data item's key.

Structure:

The list data items are stored in ascending order based on their keys. For each list data item *i*, the data item that precedes *i* has a key that is less than *i*'s key and the data item that follows *i* has a key that is greater than *i*'s key. The cursor in a nonempty list always marks one of the list's items. You iterate through the list using operations that change the position of the cursor.

Operations:

`OrderedList ( int maxNumber = MAX_LIST_SIZE )`

Requirements:
None

Results:
Constructor. Creates an empty list. Allocates enough memory for a list containing `maxNumber` data items.

`~OrderedList ()`

Requirements:
None

Results:
Destructor. Deallocates (frees) the memory used to store a list.

`void insert ( const DataType& newDataItem ) throw ( logic_error )`

Requirements:
List is not full.

Results:
Inserts `newDataItem` in its appropriate position within a list. If a data item with the same key as `newDataItem` already exists in the list, then updates that data item with `newDataItem`. Moves the cursor to mark `newDataItem`.

```
bool retrieve ( const KeyType& searchKey,
                DataType& searchDataItem ) const
```

Requirements:
None

Results:
Searches a list for the data item with key `searchKey`. If the data item is found, moves the cursor to the data item, copies it to `searchDataItem`, and returns `true`. Otherwise, returns `false` without moving the cursor and with `searchDataItem` undefined.

```
void remove () throw ( logic_error )
```

Requirements:
List is not empty.

Results:
Removes the data item marked by the cursor from a list. If the resulting list is not empty, then the cursor points to the data item that followed the deleted data item. If the deleted data item was at the end of the list, then moves the cursor to the beginning of the list.

```
void replace ( const DataType& newDataItem ) throw ( logic_error )
```

Requirements:
List is not empty.

Results:
Replaces the data item marked by the cursor with `newDataItem`. Note that this entails removing the data item at the cursor inserting `newDataItem` at the proper location. Moves the cursor to `newDataItem`.

```
void clear ()
```

Requirements:
None

Results:
Removes all the data items in a list.

```
bool isEmpty () const
```

Requirements:
None

Results:
Returns `true` if a list is empty. Otherwise, returns `false`.

```
bool isFull () const
```

Requirements:
None

Results:
Returns `true` if a list is full. Otherwise, returns `false`.

```
void gotoBeginning () throw ( logic_error )
```

Requirements:
List is not empty.

Results:
Moves the cursor to the data item at the beginning of the list.

```
void gotoEnd () throw ( logic_error )
```

Requirements:
List is not empty.

Results:
Moves the cursor to the data item at the end of the list.

```
bool gotoNext () throw ( logic_error )
```

Requirements
List is not empty.

Results:
If the cursor is not at the end of a list, then moves the cursor to the next data item in the list and returns `true`. Otherwise, returns `false`.

```
bool gotoPrior () throw ( logic_error )
```

Requirements:
List is not empty.

Results:
If the cursor is not at the beginning of a list, then moves the cursor to the preceding data item in the list and returns `true`. Otherwise, returns `false`.

```
DataType getCursor () const throw ( logic_error )
```

Requirements:
List is not empty.

Results:
Returns the value of the data item marked by the cursor.

```
void showStructure () const
```

Requirements:
None

Results:
Outputs the keys of the data items in a list. If the list is empty, outputs "Empty list". Note that this operation is intended for testing/debugging purposes only. It only supports keys that are one of C++'s predefined data types (`int`, `char`, and so forth) or for which the << operator has been overloaded.

Implementation Notes

Inheritance: The following declaration

```
class OrderedList : public List<DataType> {
    // Rest of derived class declaration here
}
```

indicates that OrderedList is derived from List. The keyword "public" specifies that this is a public inheritance—that is, OrderedList does not change List's protection mechanisms. Although rarely used, it is also possible to do "protected" or "private" inheritance, which do change the protection mechanism of the base class. We will always use public inheritance.

Access control: If you want the member functions in OrderedList to be able to refer to List's internal data members, List's data members must be declared in the protected section as shown below. If they were in the private section, OrderedList would not be able to access them.

```
class List
{
  ...

  protected:
    // Data members
    int maxSize,          // Maximum number of data items in the list
        size,             // Actual number of data items in the list
        cursor;           // Cursor array index
    DataType* dataItems;  // Array containing the list data items
};
```

Virtual functions: Recall the class declaration of List. Remember that the `insert` and `replace` member functions are declared `virtual`.

```
class List
{
  public:
    ...
    // List manipulation operations
    virtual void insert ( const DataType& newDataItem )
                      throw ( logic_error );
    virtual void replace ( const DataType& newDataItem )
                      throw ( logic_error );
    ...
};
```

We also declare `insert` and `replace` virtual in the derived class declaration.

```
class OrderedList : public List<DataType>
{
  public:
    ...
    // Modified list manipulation operations
    virtual void insert ( const DataType& newDataItem )
                        throw ( logic_error );
    virtual void replace ( const DataType& newDataItem )
                        throw ( logic_error );
    ...
};
```

Note: in both the base and the derived class, we do use the `virtual` keyword only in the class declaration, not in the class implementation.

Multiple template parameters: Template classes can have multiple generic data types. In the OrderedList, the key type is a second generic type. The syntax is to add a second parameter to the template list. As an example, the insert function implementation would begin as follows.

```
template < typename DataType, typename KeyType >
void OrderedList<DataType,KeyType>::insert(const DataType& newDataItem)
        throw ( logic_error )
```

Note that the second template type appears in two places.

1. template <typename DataType, typename KeyType>
2. OrderedList<DataType,KeyType>::

Base class constructors: In a derived class constructor, you indicate which base class constructor to use through member initialization. The format is to identify the specific constructor by passing parameters that will match the correct base class constructor. For example, in the OrderedList constructor, we wish to pass the maximum size of the list to the List constructor. We do so as follows.

```
template < typename DataType, typename KeyType >
OrderedList<DataType,KeyType>:: OrderedList ( int maxNumber )
  : List<DataType>(maxNumber)
{
    // Empty body: all initialization is done by the base class
    // constructor
}
```

Templates and accessing base class members: Inheritance gives a derived class access to all base class member functions and data that are in the public or protected sections. In C++, references to base class members from the derived class are normally transparent. For instance, to reference the variable *size* located in the base class, code in the derived class just uses the name *size*, as though it were in the derived class. However, with templated classes, you need to prefix references to base class members with scope resolution information. So to reference the *size* variable, you would need to type the following every time you reference *size*.

```
List<DataType>::size
```

To avoid having to prefix every reference to *size* with the string "List<DataType>::",
you can type the following once in the derived class declaration (in *OrderedList.h*) and
then use *size* without scope resolution syntax.

```
using List<DataType>::size;
```

This must be repeated for each base class member that is to be referenced transparently
within the derived class.

Using a key field: The following example illustrates how to declare an appropriate data
type to be used with the ordered list. It meets the Ordered List `DataType` requirements
because it has both a key field (`accountNum`) and a `getKey` function that returns the
value of the key field. All other labs with a `KeyType` have the same requirements.

```
// lab4-example1.cpp

#include "OrderedList.cpp"
class Account {
  public:
      int accountNum;            // (Key) Account number
      float balance;             // Account balance
      int getKey () const
          { return accountNum; }  // Returns the key
};
int main()
{
    OrderedList<Account, int> accounts(20);  // List of accounts
    Account acct;                            // A single account
    // Rest of program processes accounts ...
}
```

The Account structure includes the `getKey` function that returns an account's key
field—its account number. This function is used by the OrderedList class to order the
accounts as they are inserted. Insertion is done using the OrderedList class `insert`
function, but list traversal is done using the inherited List class `gotoBeginning` and
`gotoNext` functions.

Step 1: Implement the operations in the Ordered List ADT using the array representation of a list. Base your implementation on the official declaration from the
file *OrderedList.h*.

Note that you only need to create implementations of the constructor, insert,
replace, and retrieve operations for the Ordered List ADT—the remainder of
the operations are provided or are inherited from your array implementation
of the List ADT from Lab 3. Your implementations of the insert and retrieve
operations should use the `binarySearch()` function to locate a data item.
An implementation of the binary search algorithm is given in the file
search.cpp. An implementation of the showStructure operation is given in the
file *show4.cpp*.

Step 2: Save your implementation of the Ordered List ADT in the file *OrderedList.cpp*.
Be sure to document your code.

Compilation Directions

Because of how templated classes are compiled, you compile your implementation of the Ordered List ADT by compiling *test4.cpp*, which then includes *OrderedList.cpp*.

Testing

Test your implementation of the Ordered List ADT by using the program in the file *test4.cpp*. That test program allows you to interactively test your ADT implementation using the commands in the following table.

Command	Action
+key	Insert (or update) the data item with the specified key.
?key	Retrieve the data item with the specified key and output it.
—	Remove the data item marked by the cursor.
@	Display the data item marked by the cursor.
=key	Replace the data item marked by the cursor.
N	Go to the next data item.
P	Go to the prior data item.
<	Go to the beginning of the list.
>	Go to the end of the list.
E	Report whether the list is empty.
F	Report whether the list is full.
C	Clear the list.
Q	Quit the test program.

Step 1: Download the online test plans for Lab 4.

Step 2: Prepare Test Plan 4-1 for your implementation of the Ordered List ADT. Your test plan should cover the application of each operation to data items at the beginning, middle, and end of lists (where appropriate). Complete Test Plan 4-1 by filling in the test cases, commands, and expected results.

Step 3: Execute your test plan. If you discover mistakes in your implementation, correct them and execute your test plan again.

Programming Exercise 1

When a communications site transmits a message through a network like the Internet, it does not send the message as a continuous stream of data. Instead, it divides the message into pieces, called packets. These packets are sent through the network to a receiving site, which reassembles the message. Packets may travel to the receiving site along different paths. As a result, they often arrive out of sequence. In order for the receiving site to reassemble the message correctly, each packet must include the relative position of the packet within the original message. This identifier is called the sequence number.

For example, if we break the message "A SHORT MESSAGE" into packets each holding five characters and preface each packet with a number denoting the packet's position in the message, the result is the following set of packets.

```
1A SHO
2RT ME
3SSAGE
```

No matter in what order these packets arrive, a receiving site can correctly reassemble the message by placing the packets in ascending order based on their position numbers.

Step 1: Create a program that simulates reassembling an incorrectly sequenced message by reading in the packets from a text file, resequencing them, and outputting the original message. Your program should use the Ordered List ADT to assist in reassembling the packet. Each packet in the message file contains a position number and five characters from the message (the packet format shown previously). Ideally, you would base your program on the following declarations.

```
class Packet {
  public:
    static const int PACKET_SIZE = 6;  // Number of characters in a packet
                             // including null ('\0') terminator,
                             // but excluding the key (1st char in each line).
    int position;            // (Key) Packet's position w/in message
    char body[PACKET_SIZE];  // Characters in the packet
    int getKey () const
        { return position; }   // Returns the key field
};
```

Read each successive packet in the input file into a Packet object and insert the Packet object into the ordered list. Then iterate through the entire list from beginning to end, retrieving each message and printing out the message body. Save your program in *packet.cpp*.

Step 2: Prepare a test plan for your implementation of the packet resequencer. Your test plan should be developed by visually inspecting the data file and determining the expected output. Complete Test Plan 4-2 by filling in the expected results.

Step 3: Test your program using Test Plan 4-2. The message data is in the text file *message.dat*. If you discover mistakes in your program, correct them and execute your test plan again.

Programming Exercise 2

Suppose you wish to combine the data items in two ordered lists of similar size. You could use repeated calls to the insert operation to insert the data items from one list into the other. However, the resulting process would not be very efficient. A more effective approach is to use a specialized merge operation that takes advantage of the fact that the lists are ordered.

```
void merge ( const OrderedList<DataType,KeyType>& other )
    throw ( logic_error )
```

Requirements:
The list being merged into has enough free space. The two Lists have no keys in common.

Results:
Merges the data items in `other` into this list. Does not change `other`.

Even before you begin to merge the lists, you already know how much larger the list will become (remember, no key is in both lists). By traversing the lists in parallel, starting with their highest keys and working backward, you can perform the merge in a single pass. Given two ordered lists alpha and beta containing the keys

```
alpha : a d j t
beta  : b e w
```

the call

```
alpha.merge(beta);
```

produces the following results.

```
alpha : a b d e j t w
beta  : b e w
```

Step 1: Implement this operation and add it to the file *OrderedList.cpp*. A prototype for this operation is included in the declaration of the Ordered List class in the file *OrderedList.h*.

Step 2: Activate Test 1 in the test program *test4.cpp* by changing the definition of LAB4_TEST1 in *config.h* from 0 to 1 and recompiling.

Step 3: Prepare Test Plan 4-3 (merge operation) that covers lists of various lengths, including empty lists and lists that combine to produce a full list.

Step 4: Execute your test plan. If you discover mistakes in your implementation of the merge operation, correct them and execute your test plan again.

Programming Exercise 3

A set of objects can be represented in many ways. If you use an unordered list to represent a set, then performing set operations such as intersection, union, difference, and subset require up to $O(N^2)$ time. By using an ordered list to represent a set, however, you can reduce the execution time for these set operations to $O(N)$, a substantial improvement.

Consider the subset operation described below. If the sets are stored as unordered lists, this operation requires that you traverse the list once for *each* data item in other. But if the sets are stored as ordered lists, only a single traversal is required. The key is to move through the lists in parallel.

```
bool subset ( const OrdList& other ) const
```

Requirements:
None

Results:
Returns true if every key in other is also in this list. Otherwise, returns false. Does not change other.

Given four ordered lists alpha, beta, gamma, and delta containing the keys

```
alpha : a b c d
beta  : a c x
gamma : a b
delta : <empty list>
```

the function call alpha.subset(beta) yields the value false (beta is not a subset of alpha), the call alpha.subset(gamma) yields the value true (gamma is a subset of alpha), and the calls alpha.subset(delta) and beta.subset(delta) yield the value true (the empty set is a subset of every set).

Step 1: Implement this operation and add it to the file *OrderedList.cpp*. A prototype for this operation is included in the declaration of the Ordered List class in the file *OrderedList.h*.

Step 2: Activate Test 2 in the test program *test4.cpp* by changing the definition of LAB4_TEST2 in *config.h* from 0 to 1 and recompiling.

Step 3: Prepare Test Plan 4-4 for the subset operation that covers lists of various lengths, including empty lists.

Step 4: Execute your test plan. If you discover mistakes in your implementation of the subset operation, correct them and execute your test plan again.

Analysis Exercise 1

Part A

Given an ordered list containing N data items, develop worst-case, order-of-magnitude estimates of the execution time of the steps in the insert operation, assuming this operation is implemented using an array in conjunction with a binary search. Briefly explain your reasoning behind each estimate.

Array Implementation of the Insert Operation

Find the insertion point   O(   )

Insert the data item   O(   )

_____

Entire operation   O(   )

Explanation:

Part B

Suppose you had implemented the Ordered List ADT using a linear search, rather than a binary search. Given an ordered list containing N data items, develop worst-case, order-of-magnitude estimates of the execution time of the steps in the insert operation. Briefly explain your reasoning behind each estimate.

Linked List Implementation of the Insert Operation

Find the insertion point   O(   )

Insert the data item   O(   )

_____

Entire operation   O(   )

Explanation:

Analysis Exercise 2

In specifying the Ordered List ADT, we assumed that no two data items in an ordered list have the same key. What changes would you have to make to your implementation of the Ordered List ADT in order to support ordered lists in which multiple data items have the same key?

Singly Linked List Implementation of the List ADT

In this laboratory you

- implement the List ADT using a singly linked list.

- learn how to implement linked data structures using C++ pointers.

- examine how a fresh perspective on insertion and deletion can produce more efficient linked list implementations of these operations.

- learn how to use C++ inner classes.

- analyze the efficiency of your singly linked list implementation of the List ADT.

ADT Overview

In Laboratory 3, you created an implementation of the List ADT using an array to store the list data items. Although this approach is intuitive, it is not terribly efficient either in terms of memory usage or time. It wastes memory by allocating an array that is large enough to store what you estimate to be the maximum number of data items a list will ever hold. In most cases, the list is rarely this large and the extra memory simply goes unused. In addition, the insertion and deletion operations require shifting data items back and forth within the array, a very inefficient task.

In this laboratory, you implement the List ADT using a singly linked list. This implementation allocates memory data-item-by-data-item as data items are added to the list. In this way, you only allocate memory when you actually need it. Because memory is allocated over time, however, the data items do not occupy a contiguous set of memory locations. As a result, you need to link the data items together to form a linked list, as shown in the following figure.

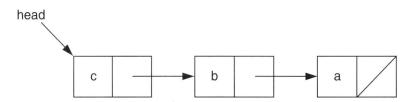

Equally important, a linked list can be reconfigured following an insertion or deletion simply by changing one or two links.

C++ Concepts Overview

Linked data structures: To implement a linked list, we need a mechanism to connect the individual data items together; pointers are the C++ method. A pointer refers to a specific location in memory where another object is stored[1]. Each pointer has a specific type that limits the type of the objects it is allowed to refer to.

Each element in the list is called a node and contains the data item and a pointer to the next node. The last node in the list has no successor, which raises the problem of what we should do with the node's pointer when there is no successor. The standard solution in computer science is to have a special value called null, which indicates that the pointer doesn't point to an object.

In contrast to the array-based list implementation, the default linked list constructor does not allocate any memory for data items; individual nodes are created as they are needed. In a similar manner, the destructor must destroy each of the nodes, one-by-one, to ensure that all dynamically allocated memory is returned to the memory manager.

Inner classes: The singly-linked list is composed of two classes, the List class and the ListNode class. There are two choices about where to declare the ListNode:

1. Using the techniques that we have learned, we can create the ListNode as a separate ADT. This becomes problematic because the List needs access to the

---

[1]Technically, a pointer can refer to objects, built-in data types, or even functions. When we say "object" when talking about what a pointer references, we intend it in the most generic sense.

ListNode, but no other classes should be allowed access. Restricting access to the ListNode can be accomplished by declaring the List class to be a friend of the ListNode class and placing the entire ListNode implementation inside the private section of the ListNode.

2. A more elegant solution involves declaring the ListNode class inside the private section of the List class. That provides encapsulation against external access, but still provides the List class with proper access.

List ADT Specification

Data items

The data items in a list are of generic type DataType.

Structure

The data items form a linear structure in which list data items follow one after the other, from the beginning of the list to its end. The ordering of the data items is determined by when and where each data item is inserted into the list and is *not* a function of the data contained in the list data items. At any point in time, one data item in any nonempty list is marked using the list's cursor. You travel through the list using operations that change the position of the cursor.

ListNode Operations

```
ListNode( const DataType& nodeData, ListNode* nextPtr )
```

Requirements:
None

Results:
Constructor. Creates an initialized ListNode by setting the ListNode's data item to the value `nodeData` and the ListNode's next pointer to the value of `nextPtr`.

List Operations

```
List ( int ignored = 0 )
```

Requirements:
None

Results:
Constructor. Creates an empty list. The parameter is provided for call compatibility with the array implementation and is ignored.

```
List ( const List& other )
```

Requirements:
None

Results:
Copy constructor. Initializes the list to be equivalent to the `other` List.

```
List& operator= ( const List& other )
```

Requirements
None

Results:
Overloaded assignment operator. Sets the list to be equivalent to the `other` List and returns a reference to this object.

```
~List ()
```

Requirements:
None

Results:
Destructor. Deallocates (frees) the memory used to store the nodes in the list.

```
void insert ( const DataType& newDataItem ) throw ( logic_error )
```

Requirements:
List is not full.

Results:
Inserts `newDataItem` into the list. If the list is not empty, then inserts `newDataItem` after the cursor. Otherwise, inserts `newDataItem` as the first (and only) data item in the list. In either case, moves the cursor to `newDataItem`.

```
void remove () throw ( logic_error )
```

Requirements:
List is not empty.

Results:
Removes the data item marked by the cursor from the list. If the resulting list is not empty, then moves the cursor to the data item that followed the deleted data item. If the deleted data item was at the end of the list, then moves the cursor to the beginning of the list.

```
void replace ( const DataType& newDataItem ) throw ( logic_error )
```

Requirements:
List is not empty.

Results:
Replaces the data item marked by the cursor with `newDataItem`. The cursor remains at `newDataItem`.

```
void clear ()
```

Requirements:
None

Results:
Removes all the data items in the list.

```
bool isEmpty () const
```

Requirements:
None

Results:
Returns `true` if the list is empty. Otherwise, returns `false`.

```
bool isFull () const
```

Requirements:
None

Results:
Returns `true` if the list is full. Otherwise, returns `false`. (Note: the implementation notes discuss the issue of what it means to say that a list of dynamically allocated nodes is full.)

```
void gotoBeginning () throw ( logic_error )
```

Requirements:
List is not empty.

Results:
Moves the cursor to the beginning of the list.

```
void gotoEnd () throw ( logic_error )
```

Requirements:
List is not empty.

Results:
Moves the cursor to the end of the list.

```
bool gotoNext () throw ( logic_error )
```

Requirements:
List is not empty.

Results:
If the cursor is not at the end of the list, then moves the cursor to mark the next data item in the list and returns `true`. Otherwise, returns `false`.

```
bool gotoPrior () throw ( logic_error )
```

Requirements:
List is not empty.

Results:
If the cursor is not at the beginning of the list, then moves the cursor to mark the preceding data item in the list and returns `true`. Otherwise, returns `false`.

```
DataType getCursor () const throw ( logic_error )
```

Requirements
List is not empty.

Results:
Returns the value of the data item marked by the cursor.

```
void showStructure () const
```

Requirements:
None

Results:
Outputs the data items in the list. If the list is empty, outputs "Empty list". Note that this operation is intended for testing/debugging purposes only. It only supports list data items that are one of C++'s predefined data types (`int`, `char`, and so forth) or other data structures with an overridden ostream `operator<<`.

Implementation Notes

Pointers: There are two main operations associated with pointers: 1) access the object being pointed to (dereference the pointer), and 2) point to an object by obtaining the object's address. A pointer is dereferenced by prefixing the pointer name with the `*` operator. To obtain the address of an object, prefix the object name with the `&` operator.

When we dereference a pointer to a class instance, we usually are trying to access member data. The syntax for doing so is `(*pointer).member`. The pointer is first dereferenced to access the object, then the specific member in the object is accessed. Parentheses are needed because the '.' operator has higher precedence than the `*` operator. Dereferencing pointers to access object members is so common that C++ provides shortcut syntax: `pointer->member`.

Null pointers in C++ are indicated by the value 0. In C, null pointers are indicated by the identifier NULL. Many individuals learned C, then C++, and have carried over the habit of using NULL. This usually works, but can cause hard-to-identify problems in certain situations, so we recommend using 0 for null at all times.

The C++ compiler provides every object with a pointer to itself named `this` and can be used like any other pointer. We can uniquely identify an object using `this` because only one object can occupy a given memory location. We compare `this` to the address of other objects in the overloaded assignment operator in order to avoid trying to copy from ourselves because the first step is usually to delete the old data to make room for the new data. If we are copying from ourselves, deleting the old data also deletes the new data.

Inner classes: The ListNode class is declared inside the List class. For example,

```
class List {
       . . .
     private:
       class ListNode {
           . . .
       };
};
```

The practical consequence of having an inner class is that the scope resolution operator must include both the outer and inner class names. For example, when defining the ListNode constructor, the function should look like the following:

```
template <typename DataType>
List<DataType>::ListNode::ListNode(const DataType& nodeData,
                                   ListNode* nextPtr)
{
     // Your implementation here
}
```

Creating new ListNode objects: The ListNode class constructor is used to add nodes to the list. The statement below, for example, creates the first node in the list with `newDataItem` as its data member.

```
head = new ListNode<DataType>(newDataItem, 0);
```

Note: The null pointer indicates that the node has no successor.

The `new` operator allocates memory for a linked list node and calls the ListNode constructor, passing both the data item to be inserted (`newDataItem`) and a pointer to the next node in the list (`0`). Finally, the assignment operator assigns a pointer to the newly allocated node to `head`, thereby completing the creation of the node.

Running out of dynamically allocated (heap) memory: The memory manager does not have an infinite amount of memory available. If a process makes a very large number of memory requests (using the `new` operator) without returning enough memory (using `delete`), it is possible to run out of memory in the heap. Approaches to determining whether there is still available memory are generally non-trivial and implementation dependent. We wish to keep the linked implementation of the List interface-compatible with the array implementation, so we need to keep the `isFull` member function. Because your applications will probably not require much memory, we recommend that your implementation of the `isFull` function assume that there is always more memory available and always return `true`. Warning: although useful for the purposes of this book, this is not an appropriate solution in many cases.

Step 1: Implement the operations in the List ADT using a singly linked list. Each node in the linked list should contain a list data item (`dataItem`) and a pointer to the node containing the next data item in the list (`next`). Your implementation should also maintain pointers to the node at the beginning of the list (`head`) and the node containing the data item marked by the cursor (`cursor`). Base your implementation on the declarations from the file *ListLinked.h*. An implementation of the showStructure operation is given in the file *show5.cpp*. Please insert the contents of *show5.cpp* into your *ListLinked.cpp* file.

Step 2: Save your implementation of the List ADT in the file *ListLinked.cpp*. Be sure to document your code.

Compilation Directions

Compile *test5.cpp*. As in previous cases with templated classes, the test program directly includes the class definition (implementation in the *.cpp* file), so it is not necessary to compile the class separately.

Testing

Test your implementation of the List ADT using the test program in the file *test5.cpp*. This program allows you to interactively test your implementation of the List ADT using the following commands.

Command	Action
+x	Insert data item *x* after the cursor.
−	Remove the data item marked by the cursor.
=x	Replace the data item marked by the cursor with data item *x*.
@	Display the data item marked by the cursor.
N	Go to the next data item.
P	Go to the prior data item.
<	Go to the beginning of the list.
>	Go to the end of the list.
E	Report whether the list is empty.
F	Report whether the list is full.
C	Clear the list.
Q	Quit the test program.

Step 1: Download the online test plans for Lab 5.

Step 2: Complete Test Plan 5-1 by adding test cases that check whether you correctly implemented the List ADT operations.

Step 3: Execute Test Plan 5-1. If you discover mistakes in your implementation of the List ADT, correct them and execute your test plan again.

Step 4: Activate Test 1 by changing the value of LAB5_TEST1 from 0 to 1 in the *config.h* file. The second test changes the data type being used by the List from a character to an integer.

Step 5: Recompile the test program. Note that recompiling this program will compile your implementation of the List ADT to produce an implementation for a list of integers.

Step 6: Replace the character data in your test plan with integer values to create Test Plan 5-2.

Step 7: Complete and execute your Test Plan 5-2 using the revised test program. If you discover mistakes in your implementation of the List ADT, correct them and execute Test Plan 5-2 again.

Programming Exercise 1

List data items need not be one of C++'s built-in types. The following declaration, for example, represents a slide show presentation as a list of slides

```
List<Slide> slideShow;
```

where each slide is an object in the Slide class outlined here.

```
class Slide
{
  public:
    static const int HEIGHT = 10,        // Slide dimensions
                     WIDTH  = 36;
    void display () const;               // Display slide and pause
  private:
    char image [HEIGHT][WIDTH];          // Slide image
    int pause;                           // Seconds to pause after
                                         //  displaying slide
    friend istream& operator>> (istream& in, Slide& slide);
    friend ostream& operator<< (ostream& out, const Slide& slide);
};
```

Step 1: Using the program shell given in the file *slideshow.cs* as a basis, create a program that reads a list of slides from a file and displays the resulting slide show from beginning to end. Your program should pause for the specified length of time after displaying each slide. It then should clear the screen (by scrolling, if necessary) before displaying the next slide.

Assume that the file containing the slide show consists of repetitions of the following slide descriptor,

Time
Row 1
Row 2
...
Row 10

where Time is the length of time to pause after displaying a slide (in seconds) and Rows 1–10 form a slide image (each row is 36 characters long).

Step 2: Test your program using Test Plan 5-3 and the slide show in the file *slides.dat*.

Programming Exercise 2

In many applications, the order of the data items in a list changes over time. Not only are new data items added and existing ones removed, but data items are repositioned within the list. The following List ADT operation moves a data item to the beginning of a list.

```
void moveToBeginning () throw ( logic_error )
```

Requirements:
List is not empty.

Results:
Removes the data item marked by the cursor from the list and reinserts the data item at the beginning of the list. Moves the cursor to the beginning of the list.

Step 1: Implement the operation described above and add it to the file *ListLinked.cpp*. A prototype for this operation is included in the declaration of the List class in the file *ListLinked.h*.

Step 2: Activate Test 2 in the test program *test5.cpp* by changing the definition of LAB5_TEST2 from 0 to 1 in *config.h* and recompiling.

Step 3: Complete Test Plan 5-4 by adding test cases that check whether your implementation of the moveToBeginning operation correctly processes requests for a number of scenarios. The test program uses M to execute the moveToBeginning operation.

Step 4: Execute Test Plan 5-4. If you discover mistakes in your implementation of the moveToBeginning operation, correct them and execute your test plan again.

Programming Exercise 3

Sometimes a more effective approach to a problem can be found by looking at the problem a little differently. Consider the following List ADT operation.

```
void insertBefore ( const DataType& newDataItem )
     throw ( logic_error )
```

Requirements:
List is not full.

Results:
Inserts `newDataItem` into a list. If the list is not empty, then inserts `newDataItem` immediately before the cursor. Otherwise, inserts `newDataItem` as the first (and only) data item in the list. In either case, moves the cursor to `newDataItem`.

You can implement this operation using a singly linked list in two very different ways. The obvious approach is to iterate through the list from its beginning until you reach the node immediately before the cursor and then to insert `newDataItem` between this node and the cursor. A more efficient approach is to copy the data item pointed to by the cursor into a new node, to insert this node after the cursor, and to place `newDataItem` in the node pointed to by the cursor. This approach is more efficient because it does not require you to iterate through the list searching for the data item immediately before the cursor.

Step 1: Implement the insertBefore operation using the second (more efficient) approach and add it to the file *ListLinked.cpp.* A prototype for this operation is included in the declaration of the List class in the file *ListLinked.h.*

Step 2: Activate Test 3 in the test program in *test5.cpp* by changing the definition of LAB5_TEST3 from 0 to 1 in *config.h* and recompiling.

Step 3: Complete Test Plan 5-5 by adding test cases that check whether your implementation of the insertBefore operation correctly handles insertions into single-data item lists and empty lists. The test program uses # to execute the insertBefore operation.

Step 4: Execute Test Plan 5-5. If you discover mistakes in your implementation of the insertBefore operation, correct them and execute your test plan again.

Analysis Exercise 1

Given a list containing N data items, develop worst-case, order-of-magnitude estimates of the execution time of the following List ADT operations, assuming they are implemented using a linked list. Briefly explain your reasoning behind each estimate.

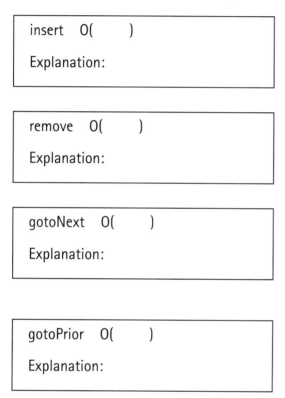

```
insert   O(     )

Explanation:
```

```
remove   O(     )

Explanation:
```

```
gotoNext   O(     )

Explanation:
```

```
gotoPrior   O(     )

Explanation:
```

Analysis Exercise 2

Part A

Programming Exercise 3 introduces a pair of approaches for implementing an insertBefore operation. One approach is straightforward, whereas the other is somewhat less obvious but more efficient. Describe how you might apply the latter approach to the remove operation. Use a diagram to illustrate your answer.

Part B

The resulting implementation of the remove operation has a worst-case, order of magnitude performance estimate of $O(N)$. Does this estimate accurately reflect the performance of this implementation? Explain why or why not.

Stack ADT

In this laboratory you

- use an abstract base class as an ADT interface.

- create two implementations of the Stack ADT—one using an array representation of stack, the other using a singly linked list representation.

- analyze the kinds of permutations you can produce using a stack.

ADT Overview

Many applications that use a linear data structure do not require the full range of operations supported by the List ADT. Although you can develop these applications using the List ADT, the resulting programs are likely to be somewhat cumbersome and inefficient. An alternative approach is to define new linear data structures that support more constrained sets of operations. By carefully defining these ADTs, you can produce ADTs that meet the needs of a diverse set of applications but yield data structures that are easier to apply—and are often more efficient—than the List ADT.

The stack is one example of a constrained linear data structure. In a stack, the data items are ordered from most recently added (the top) to least recently added (the bottom). All insertions and deletions are performed at the top of the stack. You use the push operation to insert a data item onto the stack and the pop operation to remove the topmost stack data item. A sequence of pushes and pops is shown here.

Push a	*Push* b	*Push* c	*Pop*	*Pop*
		c		
	b	b	b	
a	a	a	a	a
—	—	—	—	—

These constraints on insertion and deletion produce the "last in, first out"—LIFO—behavior that characterizes a stack. Although the stack data structure is narrowly defined, it is so extensively used by systems software that support for a primitive stack is one of the basic data items of most computer architectures.

The stack is one of the most frequently used data structures. Although all programs share the same definition of stack—a sequence of homogeneous data items with insertion and removal done at one end—the type of data item stored in stacks varies from program to program. Some use stacks of integers, others use stacks of characters, floating-point numbers, points, and so forth.

C++ Concepts Overview

Abstract base classes: An abstract base class (ABC) is any class with at least one pure virtual function (see definition below). An ABC is called abstract because it cannot be directly instantiated. A common reason for creating an ABC is to specify an interface for a set of derived classes to implement. For instance, there are good reasons for implementing a stack with arrays or with linked data structures. We provide a stack ABC to specify the functionality that any implementation must provide. Then we derive the linked and array-based implementations from the stack ABC. The benefit is that code that uses a stack, but doesn't care about the stack's implementation can refer to the ABC, while the small portion of code that does care can explicitly reference the appropriate derived class.

Pure virtual function: This is a member function that is declared, but not implemented, in a base class. The function must be implemented in any derived class that will be instantiated. Because the base class does not implement any pure virtual functions, we cannot create an object of that type since there is no code for those member functions.

Stack ADT

*[handwritten margin notes: DataType * dataItems / int maxSize / int top]*

Data items:

The data items in a stack are of generic type DataType.

Structure:

The stack data items are linearly ordered from most recently added (the top) to least recently added (the bottom). Data items are inserted onto (pushed) and removed from (popped) the top of the stack.

Operations:

```
Stack ( int maxNumber = MAX_STACK_SIZE )
```

Requirements:
None

Results:
Constructor. Creates an empty stack. Allocates enough memory for a stack containing `maxNumber` data items (if necessary).[1]

```
Stack ( const Stack& other )
```

Requirements:
None

Results:
Copy constructor. Initializes the stack to be equivalent to the `other` Stack object parameter.[1]

```
Stack& operator= ( const Stack& other )
```

Requirements:
None

Results:
Overloaded assignment operator. Sets the stack to be equivalent to the `other` Stack object parameter and returns a reference to the modified stack.[2]

```
~Stack ()
```

Requirements:
None

Results:
Destructor. Deallocates (frees) the memory used to store the stack.

---

[1]Because of the way ABCs work, constructors are actually declared and implemented in the derived classes, not in the base class. This relates to the requirement that constructor names match the class names; it is impossible for the base class and the derived class to have the same name.

[2]Like ABC constructors, `operator=` is declared and implemented in the derived classes with corresponding name changes.

```
void push ( const DataType& newDataItem ) throw ( logic_error )
```

Requirements:
Stack is not full.

Results:
Inserts `newDataItem` onto the top of the stack.

```
DataType pop () throw ( logic_error )
```

Requirements:
Stack is not empty.

Results:
Removes the most recently added (top) data item from the stack and returns the value of the deleted item.

```
void clear ()
```

Requirements:
None

Results:
Removes all the data items in the stack.

```
bool isEmpty () const
```

Requirements:
None

Results:
Returns `true` if the stack is empty. Otherwise, returns `false`.

```
bool isFull () const
```

Requirements:
None

Results:
Returns true if the stack is `full`. Otherwise, returns `false`.

```
void showStructure () const
```

Requirements:
None

Results:
Outputs the data items in a stack. If the stack is empty, outputs "Empty stack". Note that this operation is intended for testing/debugging purposes only. It only supports stack data items that are one of C++'s predefined data types (`int`, `char`, and so forth) or other data structures with an overridden ostream `operator<<`.

Implementation Notes

Pure virtual function: A member function is identified as a pure virtual function in the class declaration by the word `virtual`, followed by the class prototype, followed by the string "=0". For instance, the Stack ABC `isEmpty` function is declared as follows:

```
virtual bool isEmpty() const = 0;
```

Stack implementations: Multiple versions of an ADT may be necessary if the ADT is to perform efficiently in a variety of operating environments. Depending on the hardware and the application, you may want an implementation that reduces the execution time of some (or all) of the ADT operations, or you may want an implementation that reduces the amount of memory used to store the ADT data items. In this laboratory, you develop two implementations of the Stack ADT. One implementation stores the stack in an array, the other stores each data item separately and links the data items together to form a stack.

Array-Based Implementation

Step 1: Implement the operations in the Stack ADT using an array to store the stack data items. Stacks change in size, therefore you need to store the maximum number of data items the stack can hold (`maxSize`) and the array index of the topmost data item in the stack (`top`), along with the stack data items themselves (`dataItems`). Base your implementation on the declarations from the file *StackArray.h*. An implementation of the showStructure operation is given in the file *show6.cpp*.

Step 2: Save your array implementation of the Stack ADT in the file *StackArray.cpp*. Be sure to document your code.

Compilation Directions

Compile test6.cpp. The value of LAB6_TEST1 in *config.h* determines whether the array-based implementation or the linked-list implementation is tested. If the value is 0 (the default), the array implementation is tested. If the value is 1, then the linked implementation is tested.

Testing

Test your implementation of the array-based Stack ADT using the program in the file *test6.cpp*. The test program allows you to interactively test your ADT implementation using the commands in the following table.

Command	Action
+x	Push data item x onto the top of the stack.
–	Pop the top data item and output it.
E	Report whether the stack is empty.
F	Report whether the stack is full.
C	Clear the stack.
Q	Exit the test program.

Step 1: Download the online test plans for Lab 6.

Step 2: Complete the test plan for Test 6-1 by filling in the expected results for each given operation. Add test cases in which you

- pop a data item from a stack containing only one data item,
- push a data item onto a stack that has been emptied by a series of pops,
- pop a data item from a full stack (array implementation), and
- clear the stack.

Step 3: Execute Test Plan 6-1. If you discover mistakes in your implementation of the Stack ADT, correct them and execute the test plan again.

Linked-List Implementation

In your array implementation of the Stack ADT, you allocate the memory used to store a stack when the stack is declared (constructed). The resulting array must be large enough to hold the largest stack you might possibly need in a particular application. Unfortunately, most of the time the stack will not actually be this large and the extra memory will go unused.

An alternative approach is to allocate memory data item-by-data item as new data items are added to the stack. In this way, you only allocate memory when you actually need it. Because memory is allocated over time, however, the data items do not occupy a contiguous set of memory locations. As a result, you need to link the data items together to form a linked list representation of a stack, as shown in the following figure.

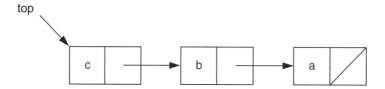

Creating a linked list implementation of the Stack ADT presents a somewhat more challenging programming task than did developing an array implementation. One way to simplify this task is to divide the implementation into two template classes: one focusing on the overall stack structure (the Stack class) and another focusing on the individual nodes in the linked list (the StackNode class).

Let's begin with the StackNode class. Each node in the linked list contains a stack data item and a pointer to the node containing the next data item in the list. The only function provided by the StackNode class is a constructor that creates a specified node.

Access to the StackNode class is restricted to member functions of the Stack class. Other classes are blocked from referencing linked list nodes directly by declaring the StackNode as an inner class of Stack. (Refer to the Lab 5 C++ concepts and implementation sections for details.)

The StackNode class constructor is used to add nodes to the stack. The statement below, for example, adds a node containing `newDataItem` ('d' in this example) to a stack of characters. Note that `top` is of type `StackNode*`.

```
top = new StackNode<DataType>(newDataItem,top);
```

The `new` operator allocates memory for a linked list node and calls the StackNode constructor passing both the data item to be inserted ('d') and a pointer to the next node in the list (`top`).

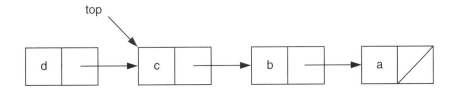

Finally, the assignment operator assigns a pointer to the newly allocated node to `top`, thereby completing the creation and linking of the node.

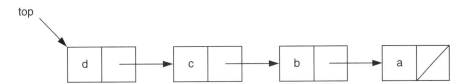

The member functions of the Stack class implement the operations in the Stack ADT. A pointer is maintained to the node at the beginning of the linked list or, equivalently, the top of the stack. The following declaration for the Stack class is given in the file *StackLinked.h.*

Step 1: Implement the operations in the Stack ADT using a singly linked list to store the stack data items. Each node in the linked list should contain a stack data item (`dataItem`) and a pointer to the node containing the next data item in the stack (`next`). Your implementation should also maintain a pointer to the node containing the topmost data item in the stack (`top`). Base your implementation on the class declarations in the file *StackLinked.h.* A linked-list implementation of the showStructure operation is given in the file *show6.cpp.*

Step 2: Save your linked list implementation of the Stack ADT in the file *StackLinked.cpp.* Be sure to document your code.

Compilation Directions

Edit *config.h* and change the value of LAB6_TEST1 to 1. (If the value is 0, then the array-based implementation is tested instead.) Recompile *test6.cpp*.

Testing

Test your implementation of the linked list Stack ADT using the program in the file *test6.cpp*.

Step 1: Re-execute Test Plan 6-1. If you discover mistakes in your linked-list implementation of the Stack ADT, correct them and execute your test plan again.

Programming Exercise 1

We commonly write arithmetic expressions in infix form, that is, with each operator placed between its operands, as in the following expression.

$$(3 + 4) * (5 / 2)$$

Although we are comfortable writing expressions in this form, infix form has the disadvantage that parentheses must be used to indicate the order in which operators are to be evaluated. These parentheses, in turn, greatly complicate the evaluation process.

Evaluation is much easier if we can simply evaluate operators from left to right. Unfortunately, this evaluation strategy will not work with the infix form of arithmetic expressions. However, it will work if the expression is in postfix form. In the postfix form of an arithmetic expression, each operator is placed immediately after its operands. The expression above is written in postfix form as

$$3 \ 4 + 5 \ 2 \ / \ *$$

Note that both forms place the numbers in the same order (reading from left to right). The order of the operators is different, however, because the operators in the postfix form are positioned in the order that they are evaluated. The resulting postfix expression is hard to read at first, but it is easy to evaluate. All you need is a stack on which to place intermediate results.

Suppose you have an arithmetic expression in postfix form that consists of a sequence of single digit, nonnegative integers and the four basic arithmetic operators (addition, subtraction, multiplication, and division). This expression can be evaluated using the following algorithm in conjunction with a stack of floating-point numbers.

Read in the expression character-by-character. As each character is read in:

- If the character corresponds to a single digit number (characters '0' to '9'), then push the corresponding floating-point number onto the stack.
- If the character corresponds to one of the arithmetic operators (characters '+', '-', '*', and '/'), then
- Pop a number off of the stack. Call it *operand1*.
- Pop a number off of the stack. Call it *operand2*.
- Combine these operands using the arithmetic operator, as follows:
  Result = *operand2* operator *operand1*.
- Push *result* onto the stack.

When the end of the expression is reached, pop the remaining number off the stack. This number is the value of the expression.

Applying this algorithm to the arithmetic expression

$$3 \ 4 + 5 \ 2 \ / \ *$$

yields the following computation

'3' : Push 3.0

'4' : Push 4.0

'+'   :   Pop, *operand1* = 4.0

             Pop, *operand2* = 3.0

             Combine, *result* = 3.0 + 4.0 = 7.0

             Push 7.0

'5'   :   Push 5.0

'2'   :   Push 2.0

'/'   :   Pop, *operand1* = 2.0

             Pop, *operand2* = 5.0

             Combine, *result* = 5.0 / 2.0 = 2.5

             Push 2.5

'*'   :   Pop, *operand1* = 2.5

             Pop, *operand2* = 7.0

             Combine, *result* = 7.0 * 2.5 = 17.5

             Push 17.5

'\n'   :   Pop, Value of expression = 17.5

Step 1: Create a program that reads the postfix form of an arithmetic expression, evaluates it, and outputs the result. Assume that the expression consists of single-digit, nonnegative integers ('0' to '9') and the four basic arithmetic operators ('+', '-', '*', and '/'). Further assume that the arithmetic expression is input from the keyboard with all the characters separated by white space on one line. Save your program in a file called *postfix.cpp*.

Step 2: Complete Test Plan 6-2 by filling in the expected result for each arithmetic expression. You may wish to include additional arithmetic expressions in this test plan.

Step 3: Execute the test plan. If you discover mistakes in your program, correct them and execute the test plan again.

Programming Exercise 2

A classic computer science problem that can be solved with a stack is called the 8-queens problem. The question is whether it is possible to safely place eight queens on a chessboard. The answer is yes, so the question is often modified to list one or more safe scenarios.

The standard algorithm is to place a queen in a potentially safe spot and check whether it is safe. If it is safe, leave it and try placing another queen; otherwise, remove it and try placing it in another place. If no safe locations can be found, then a queen previously declared safe must also be removed. Continue until all eight queens are safely on the board. The process of trying a solution that may require undoing is called backtracking.

We use a stack to facilitate backtracking. When a queen is thought to be safely placed, we push the queen's location on to the stack. When we need to remove a queen, we pop the location from the stack.

Step 1:   Write an implementation of the previous algorithm. We provide an implementation of a number of routines to represent and manipulate the queens on the board. You must maintain the stack and track queen placement.

Step 2:   Save a copy of the file *queens.cs* as *queens.cpp*. Write your implementation of the 8-queens main algorithm in the file *queens.cpp*.

Step 3:   Compile and run the program in *queens.cpp*.

Step 4:   Visually verify that the printed solution is valid. Because visual inspection on the screen can make it hard to determine whether your solution is valid, Test Plan 6-3 is available for you to write the results if you wish.

Programming Exercise 3

One of the tasks that compilers and interpreters must frequently perform is deciding whether some pair of expression delimiters are properly paired, even if they are embedded multiple pairs deep. Consider the following C++ expression.

```
a=(f(b)-(c+d))/2;
```

The compiler has to be able to determine which pairs of opening and closing parentheses go together and whether the whole expression is correctly parenthesized. A number of possible errors can occur because of incomplete pairs of parentheses—more of one than the other—or because of improperly placed parentheses. For instance, the expression below lacks a closing parenthesis.

```
a=(f(b)-(c+d)/2;
```

A stack is extremely helpful in implementing solutions to this type of problem because of its LIFO—Last In, First Out—behavior. A closing parenthesis needs to be matched with the most recently encountered opening parenthesis. This is handled by pushing opening parentheses onto a stack as they are encountered. When a closing parenthesis is encountered, it should be possible to pop the matching opening parenthesis off the stack. If it is determined that every closing parenthesis had a matching opening parenthesis, then the expression is valid.

```
bool delimitersOk( const string& expression )
```

Requirements:
None

Results:
Returns `true` if all the parentheses and braces in the string are legally paired. Otherwise, returns `false`.

Step 1: Save a copy of the file *delimiters.cs* as *delimiters.cpp*. Implement the delimitersOk operation inside the *delimiters.cpp* program.

Step 2: Complete Test Plan 6-4 by adding test cases that check whether your implementation of the delimitersOk operation correctly detects improperly paired delimiters in input expressions. Note that it is not required that the input be valid C++ expressions, just the delimiters are correct.

Step 5: Execute your test plan. If you discover mistakes in your implementation of the delimitersOk operation, correct them and execute the test plan again.

Analysis Exercise 1

Given the input string `"abc"`, which permutations of this string can be output by a code fragment consisting of only the statement pairs

```
cin >> ch;   permuteStack.push(ch);
```

and

```
ch = permuteStack.pop();   cout << ch;
```

where `ch` is a character and `permuteStack` is a stack of characters? Note that each of the statement pairs may be repeated several times within the code fragment and that the statement pairs may be in any order. For instance, the code fragment

```
cin >> ch;   permuteStack.push(ch);
cin >> ch;   permuteStack.push(ch);
cin >> ch;   permuteStack.push(ch);
ch = permuteStack.pop();   cout << ch;
ch = permuteStack.pop();   cout << ch;
ch = permuteStack.pop();   cout << ch;
```

outputs the string `"cba"`.

Part A

For each of the permutations listed below, give a code fragment that outputs the permutation or a brief explanation of why the permutation cannot be produced.

`"abc"`	`"acb"`
`"bac"`	`"bca"`
`"cab"`	`"cba"`

Part B

Given the input string `"abcd"`, which permutations beginning with the character `'d'` can be output using the same code fragment combinations (e.g., cin/push, pop/cout) described previously? Why can only these permutations be produced?

Analysis Exercise 2

For each of the stack implementations, identify the performance order of magnitude (big-O value) for the listed operations. Then provide a justification for your big-O value.

Operation	Array–based	Linked
push	O( )	O( )
Justification		
pop	O( )	O( )
Justification		
clear	O( )	O( )
Justification		

7

Queue ADT

In this laboratory you

- create two implementations of the Queue ADT—one based on an array representation of a queue, the other based on a singly linked list representation.

- utilize a queue in a simple simulation.

- learn about pseudo random numbers.

- analyze the memory requirements of your array and linked list queue representations.

ADT Overview

This laboratory focuses on another constrained linear data structure, the queue. The data items in a queue are ordered from least recently added (the front) to most recently added (the rear). Insertions are performed at the rear of the queue and deletions are performed at the front. You use the enqueue operation to insert data items and the dequeue operation to remove data items. A sequence of enqueues and dequeues is shown here.

Enqueue a	Enqueue b	Enqueue c	Dequeue	Dequeue
a	a b	a b c	b c	c
←front	←front	←front	←front	←front

The movement of data items through a queue reflects the "first in, first out"–FIFO–behavior that is characteristic of the flow of customers in a line or the transmission of information across a data channel. Queues are routinely used to regulate the flow of physical objects, information, and requests for resources (or services) through a system. Operating systems, for example, use queues to control access to system resources such as printers, files, and communications lines. Queues also are widely used in simulations to model the flow of objects or information through a system.

C++ Concepts Overview

The Queue uses the same C++ constructs as the stack. See Laboratory 6 for details if needed.

Queue ADT

Data items:

The data items in a queue are of generic type DataType.

Structure:

The queue data items are linearly ordered from least recently added (the front) to most recently added (the rear). Data items are inserted at the rear of the queue (enqueued) and are removed from the front of the queue (dequeued).

Operations:

```
Queue ( int maxNumber = MAX_QUEUE_SIZE )
```

Requirements:
None

Results:
Constructor. Creates an empty queue. Allocates enough memory for the queue containing `maxNumber` data items (if necessary).[1]

```
Queue ( const Queue& other )
```

Requirements:
None

Results:
Copy constructor. Initializes the queue to be equivalent to the `other` Queue object parameter.[1]

```
Queue& operator= ( const Queue& other )
```

Requirements:
None

Results:
Overloaded assignment operator. Sets the queue to be equivalent to the `other` Queue object parameter and returns a reference to the modified queue.[2]

```
~Queue ()
```

Requirements:
None

Results:
Destructor. Deallocates (frees) the memory used to store the queue.

```
void enqueue ( const DataType& newDataItem ) throw ( logic_error )
```

Requirements:
Queue is not full.

Results:
Inserts `newDataItem` at the rear of the queue.

```
DataType dequeue () throw ( logic_error )
```

Requirements:
Queue is not empty.

Results:
Removes the least recently added (front) data item from the queue and returns it.

---

[1]Because of the way ABCs work, constructors are actually declared and implemented in the derived classes, not in the base class. This relates to the requirement that constructor names match the class names; it is impossible for the base class and the derived class to have the same name.

[2]Like ABC constructors, `operator=` is declared and implemented in the derived classes with corresponding name changes.

```
void clear ()
```

Requirements:
None

Results:
Removes all the data items in the queue.

```
bool isEmpty () const
```

Requirements:
None

Results:
Returns `true` if the queue is empty. Otherwise, returns `false`.

```
bool isFull () const
```

Requirements:
None

Results:
Returns `true` if the queue is full. Otherwise, returns `false`.

```
void showStructure () const
```

Requirements:
None

Results:
Outputs the data items in the queue. If the queue is empty, outputs "Empty queue". Note that this operation is intended for testing/debugging purposes only. It only supports queue data items that are one of C++'s predefined data types (int, char, and so forth) or other data structures with an overridden ostream `operator<<`.

Implementation Notes

Just like you did with the stack laboratory (Lab 6), you are to create two implementations of the Queue ADT. One of these implementations is based on an array, the other is based on a singly-linked list.

Array-Based Implementation

Step 1: Implement the operations in the Queue ADT using an array to store the queue data items. Queues change in size, therefore you need to store the maximum number of data items the queue can hold (`maxSize`) and the array index of the data items at the front and rear of the queue (`front` and `rear`), along with the queue data items themselves (dataItems). Base your implementation on the declarations from the file *QueueArray.h.* An array-based implementation of the showStructure operation is given in the file *show7.cpp.*

Step 2:   Save your array implementation of the Queue ADT in the file *QueueArray.cpp.* Be sure to document your code.

Compilation Directions

Compile *test7.cpp.* The value of LAB7_TEST1 in *config.h* determines whether the array-based implementation or the linked-list implementation is tested. If the value is 0 (the default), the array implementation is tested. If the value is 1, then the linked implementation is tested.

Testing

Test your implementation of the array-based Stack ADT using the program in the file *test7.cpp.* The test program allows you to interactively test your ADT implementation using the commands in the following table.

Command	Action
+x	Enqueue data item x.
-	Dequeue a data item and output it.
E	Report whether the queue is empty.
F	Report whether the queue is full.
C	Clear the queue.
Q	Exit the test program.

Step 1:   Download the online test plans for Lab 7.

Step 2:   Complete Test Plan 7-1 by filling in the expected results for each given operation. Add test cases in which you

- enqueue a data item onto a queue that has been emptied by a series of dequeues,
- combine enqueues and dequeues so that you "go around the end" of the array (array implementation only),
- dequeue a data item from a full queue (array implementation only), and
- clear the queue.

Step 3:   Execute Test Plan 7-1. If you discover mistakes in your implementation of the Queue ADT, correct them and execute the test plan again.

Linked–List Implementation

Step 1: Implement the operations in the Queue ADT using a singly linked list to store the queue data items. Each node in the linked list should contain a queue data item (dataItem) and a pointer to the node containing the next data item in the queue (next). Your implementation should also maintain pointers to the nodes containing the front and rear data items in the queue (front and rear). Base your implementation on the following declarations from the file *QueueLinked.h*. A linked-list implementation of the showStructure operation is given in the file *show7.cpp*.

Step 2: Save your linked list implementation of the Queue ADT in the file *QueueLinked.cpp*. Be sure to document your code.

Compilation Directions

Edit *config.h* and change the value of LAB7_TEST1 to 1. (If the value is 0, then the array-based implementation is tested instead.) Recompile *test7.cpp*.

Testing

Test your implementation of the linked list Queue ADT using the program in the file *test7.cpp*.

Step 1: Re-execute the pertinent portions of Test Plan 7-1. If you discover mistakes in your linked-list implementation of the Queue ADT, correct them and execute your test plan again.

Programming Exercise 1

In this exercise, you use a queue to simulate the flow of customers through a check-out line in a store. In order to create this simulation, you must model both the passage of time and the flow of customers through the line. You can model time using a loop in which each pass corresponds to a set time interval–1 minute, for example. You can model the flow of customers using a queue in which each data item corresponds to a customer in the line.

In order to complete the simulation, you need to know the rate at which customers join the line, as well as the rate at which they are served and leave the line. Suppose the check-out line has the following properties.

- One customer is served and leaves the line every minute (assuming there is at least one customer waiting to be served during that minute).
- Between zero and two customers join the line every minute, where there is a 50 percent chance that no customers arrive, a 25 percent chance that one customer arrives, and a 25 percent chance that two customers arrive.

You can simulate the flow of customers through the line during a time period n minutes long using the following algorithm.

Initialize the queue to empty.

While the simulation is not done

    Increment simulated time by one minute

    If the queue is not empty, then remove the customer at the front of the queue.

    Compute a random number k between 0 and 3.

    If k is 1, then add one customer to the line.

    If k is 2, then add two customers to the line.

    Otherwise (if k is 0 or 3), do not add any customers to the line.

    Update queue statistics.

Calling the `rand` function is a simple way to generate pseudo-random numbers. It should be available through the `<cstdlib>` function set. Generating random numbers does vary from platform to platform because of compiler and operating system differences. You may need to get help from your lab instructor on how to generate random numbers in your particular context.

Step 1: Using the program shell given in the file *storesim.cs* as a basis, create a program in *storesim.cpp* that uses the Queue ADT to implement the model described above. Your program should update the following information during each simulated minute.

- The total number of customers served.
- The combined length of time these customers spent waiting in line.
- The maximum length of time any of these customers spent waiting in line.

The data that is stored in the queue should contain everything that is necessary to 1) represent the customer and 2) compute the previous statistics. To compute how long a customer waited to be served, you need the difference in time from when the customer arrived to when the customer exited the queue. There is no additional information needed in the statistics, nor is there any customer-specific information that is used for our simple simulation. Therefore, we can represent the customer in the queue simply by using the simulated time the customer entered the queue.

Step 2: Use your program to simulate the flow of customers through the line and complete Table 7-2 in the online supplement. Note that the average wait is the combined waiting time divided by the total number of customers served.

Programming Exercise 2

A deque (or double-ended queue) is a linear data structure that allows data items to be inserted and removed at both ends. Adding the operations described below will transform your Queue ADT into a Deque ADT.

```
void putFront ( const DataType& newDataItem ) throw ( logic_error )
```

Requirements:
Queue is not full.

Results:
Inserts `newDataItem` at the front of the queue. The order of the preexisting data items is left unchanged.

```
DataType getRear () throw ( logic_error )
```

Requirements:
Queue is not empty.

Results:
Removes the most recently added (rear) data item from the queue and returns it. The remainder of the queue is left unchanged.

Step 1: Implement these operations using the array representation of a queue and add them to the file *QueueArray.cpp*. Prototypes for these operations are included in the declaration of the Queue class in the file *QueueArray.h*.

Step 2: Select the array implementation of Queue by setting the value of LAB7_TEST1 to 0 in *config.h*. Then activate Test 2 by changing the value of LAB7_TEST2 from 0 to 1.

Step 3: Complete Test Plan 7-3 by adding test cases in which you

- insert a data item at the front of a newly emptied queue,
- remove a data item from the rear of a queue containing only one data item,
- "go around the end" of the array using each of these operations (only the array implementation), and
- mix `putFront` and `getRear` with `enqueue` and `dequeue`. The test program uses > to execute the putFront operation and = to execute the getRear operation.

Step 4: Execute Test Plan 7-3. If you discover mistakes in your implementation of these operations, correct them and execute the test plan again.

Step 5: Select the linked implementation of Queue by changing the value of LAB7_TEST1 from 0 to 1 in *config.h*.

Step 6: Re-execute the pertinent portions of Test Plan 7-3 for your linked implementation. If you discover mistakes in your implementation of these operations, correct them and execute the test plan again.

Programming Exercise 3

When a queue is used as part of a model or simulation, the modeler is often very interested in how many data items are on the queue at various points in time. This statistic is produced by the following operation.

```
int getLength () const
```

Requirements:
None

Results:
Returns the number of data items in a queue.

Step 1: Implement these operations using the array representation of a queue and add them to the file *QueueArray.cpp*. Prototypes for these operations are included in the declaration of the Queue class in the file *QueueArray.h*.

Step 2: Select the array implementation of Queue by setting the value of LAB7_TEST1 to 0 in *config.h*. Then activate Test 3 by changing the value of LAB7_TEST3 from 0 to 1.

Step 3: Complete Test Plan 7-4 by adding test cases in which you test `getLength` with queues of various lengths. The test program uses # to execute the getLength operation.

Step 4: Execute Test Plan 7-4. If you discover mistakes in your implementation of these operations, correct them and execute the test plan again.

Step 5: Select the linked implementation of Queue by changing the value of LAB7_TEST1 from 0 to 1 in *config.h*.

Step 6: Re-execute Test Plan 7-4 for your linked implementation. If you discover mistakes in your implementation of these operations, correct them and execute the test plan again.

Analysis Exercise 1

Part A

Given the following memory requirements

Integer   4 bytes

Address (pointer)   4 bytes

and a queue containing one hundred integers, compare the amount of memory used by your array representation of the queue to the amount of memory used by your singly linked list representation. Assume that the array representation allows a queue to contain a maximum of one hundred data items.

Note: integer and pointers memory requirements vary depending on the operating system and compiler. Integers and addresses range in size from 2 to 8 bytes, or larger. The values above represent a specific platform and were chosen for simplicity of calculation.

Part B

Suppose that you have ten queues of integers. Of these ten queues, four are 50% full, and the remaining six are 10% full. Compare the amount of memory used by your array representation of these queues with the amount of memory used by your singly linked list representation. Assume that the array representation allows a queue to contain a maximum of one hundred data items.

Part C

Suppose that you have a large object that requires 1000 bytes of memory. Repeat the analysis from Part A using a queue of large objects. How does the large object affect the memory efficiency of the two queues?

Analysis Exercise 2

In Programming Exercise 1, you used a queue to simulate the flow of customers through a line. Describe another application where you might use the Queue ADT. What type of information does your application store in each queue data item?

Expression Tree ADT

In this laboratory you

- create an implementation of the Expression Tree ADT using a linked tree structure.

- use recursion to implement various operations.

- develop an implementation of the Expression Tree ADT that represents logic expressions and use your implementation to model a simple logic circuit.

- learn how to use C++ template specialization.

- analyze how preorder, inorder, and postorder tree traversals are used in your implementation of the Expression Tree ADT.

Objectives

ADT Overview

Although you ordinarily write arithmetic expressions in linear form, you treat them as hierarchical entities when you evaluate them. For example, when evaluating the following arithmetic expression,

```
( 1 + 3 ) * ( 6 - 4 )
```

you first add 1 and 3, then you subtract 4 from 6. Finally, you multiply these intermediate results together to produce the value of the expression. In performing these calculations, you have implicitly formed a hierarchy in which the multiply operator is built upon a foundation consisting of the addition and subtraction operators. You can represent this hierarchy explicitly using the following binary tree. Trees such as this one are referred to as expression trees.

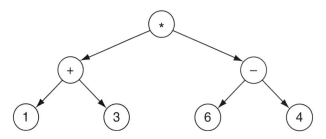

C++ Concepts Overview

Template specialization: In developing template classes, we must implement the class so that it works for all possible data types. It may be the case that some data types could be implemented more efficiently. For example, the List ADT could be implemented "specially" for the `bool` type since we could pack multiple `bool` values into a single `int`. Template specialization allows you to provide an implementation of the template class for a specific data type.

Reference pointers: Pointers and references do not have to be mutually exclusive choices. We can have a reference to a pointer, which can be useful as a parameter to a function. By making a parameter a reference, all changes to the formal parameter are reflected in the actual parameter. This enables creating a parameter that points to an element, but that may point to a different element by the end of a function call.

Expression Tree ADT

Data items:

Each node in an expression tree contains either an arithmetic operator or a numeric value.

Structure:

The nodes form a tree in which each node containing an arithmetic operator has a pair of children. Each child is the root node of a subtree that represents one of the operator's operands. Nodes containing numeric values have no children.

Operations

`ExprTree ()`

Requirements:
None

Results:
Constructor. Creates an empty expression tree.

`ExprTree ( const ExprTree& other )`

Requirements:
None

Results:
Copy constructor. Initializes the expression tree to be equivalent to the `other` ExprTree object parameter.

`ExprTree& operator= ( const ExprTree& other )`

Requirements:
None

Results:
Overloaded assignment operator. Sets the expression tree to be equivalent to the `other` ExprTree object parameter and returns a reference to this object.

`~ExprTree ()`

Requirements:
None

Results:
Destructor. Deallocates (frees) the memory used to store the expression tree.

`void build ()`

Requirements:
None

Results:
Reads an arithmetic expression in prefix form from the keyboard and builds the corresponding expression tree.

```
void expression () const
```

Requirements:
None

Results:
Outputs the expression corresponding to the value of the tree in fully parenthesized infix form.

```
DataType evaluate () const throw ( logic_error )
```

Requirements:
Expression tree is not empty.

Results:
Returns the value of the corresponding arithmetic expression.

```
void clear ()
```

Requirements:
None

Results:
Removes all the data items in the expression tree.

```
void showStructure () const
```

Requirements:
None

Results:
Outputs an expression tree with its branches oriented from left (root) to right (leaves)—that is, the tree output is rotated counterclockwise ninety degrees from its conventional orientation. If the tree is empty, outputs "Empty tree". Note that this operation is intended for testing/debugging purposes only. It assumes that arithmetic expressions contain only single-digit, nonnegative integers and the arithmetic operators for addition, subtraction, multiplication, and division.

Implementation Notes

Prefix notation: We commonly write arithmetic expressions in infix form—that is, with each operator placed between its operands, as in the following expression.

```
( 1 + 3) * ( 6 - 4 )
```

In this laboratory, you construct an expression tree from the prefix form of an arithmetic expression. In prefix form, each operator is placed immediately before its operands. The previous expression is written in prefix form as

```
* + 1 3 - 6 4
```

When processing the prefix form of an arithmetic expression from left to right, you will, by definition, encounter each operator followed by its operands. If you know in advance the number of operands that an operator has, you can use the following recursive process to construct the corresponding expression tree.

```
Read the next arithmetic operator or numeric value.
Create a node containing the operator or numeric value.
if the node contains an operator
    then Recursively build the subtrees that correspond to the
        operator's operands.
    else The node is a leaf node.
```

If you apply this process to the arithmetic expression

```
* + 1 3 - 6 4
```

then construction of the corresponding expression tree proceeds as follows:

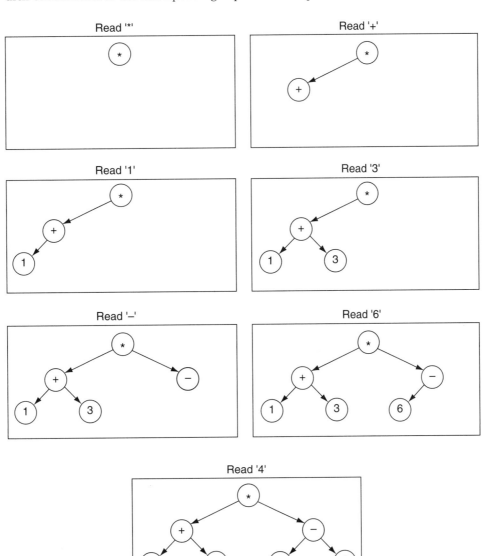

Helper functions: With functions that are naturally implemented using recursion, it is useful to have a separate function that provides a public interface to the class. That function then calls a private "helper" function with a set of appropriate parameters. The helper function performs the recursive work, while the public interface function ensures that the recursive process gets started correctly and any return value is sent back to the caller.

Template Specialization: To define the implementation of a specialized class, you must indicate that the implementation refers to a specific data type for a template. You do this by prefixing the class with "`template <>`" and adding the type to the class name. For example, to specialize the List class for the `bool` datatype, you would do as follows.

```
template<>
class List<bool> {
    . . .
}
```

You may also specialize an individual function within a templated class. We do this in the expression tree ADT because the evaluation of an expression tree depends on the data type that it holds. We initially specialize the `evalHelper` function for float values, then add a specialized `evalHelper` to support `bool` values in programming Exercise 1. You specialize a function similarly to specializing a class. The following code specializes the `evalHelper` function for cases when `DataType` is `float`.

```
template <>
float ExprTree<float>::evalHelper(ExprTreeNode* p) const {
    . . . // Use float instead of DataType here
}
```

Reference pointers: To define a parameter that is a reference to a pointer, you simply use both the `&` and `*` in the data type specification for the parameter. For example, the following code declares the helper function (`buildHelper`) for the `build` function. The function takes a reference to a pointer to an expression tree node so that if a new node should be added to the tree, it can be allocated and added by simply assigning the newly allocated node to the `node` parameter.

```
template<typename DataType>
void ExprTree<DataType>::buildHelper(ExprTreeNode*& node) {
    . . .
}
```

Note: the order of the `*` and `&` operators is significant. "`*&`" means a reference to a pointer, but "`&*`" means a pointer to a reference, which is nonsense to the compiler.

Step 1:   Implement the operations in Expression Tree ADT using a linked tree structure. Assume that an arithmetic expression consists of single-digit, nonnegative integers (`'0'..'9'`) and the four basic arithmetic operators (`'+'`, `'-'`, `'*'` and `'/'`). Further assume that each arithmetic expression is input in prefix form from the keyboard with all of the characters separated by whitespace on one line.

As with the linear linked structures you developed in prior laboratories, your implementation of the linked tree structure uses a pair of classes: one for the nodes in the tree (ExprTreeNode) and one for the overall tree structure (ExprTree). Each node in the tree should contain a character (dataItem) and a pair of pointers to the node's children (left and right). Your Expression Tree implementation should also maintain a pointer to the tree's root node (root). Base your implementation on the declarations from the file *ExprTree.h*. An implementation of the showStructure operation is given in the file *show8.cpp*.

Step 2: The declaration of the ExprTree class in the file *ExprTree.h* does not include prototypes for the private recursive helper functions needed by your implementation of the Expression Tree ADT. Add these prototypes to the file *ExprTree.h*.

Step 3: Save your implementation of the Expression Tree ADT in the file *ExprTree.cpp*. Be sure to document your code.

Compilation Directions

Step 1: Compile the test program in the file *test8.cpp*.

Testing

Test your implementation of the Expression Tree ADT using the test program in the file *test8.cpp*.

Step 1: Complete Test Plan 8-1 by filling in the expected result for each arithmetic expression. You may wish to add arithmetic expressions to the test plan.

Step 2: Execute Test Plan 8-1. If you discover mistakes in your implementation of the Expression Tree ADT, correct them and execute the test plan again.

Programming Exercise 1

Computers are composed of logic circuits that take a set of boolean input values and produce a boolean output. You can represent this mapping from inputs to output with a logic expression consisting of the boolean logic operators AND, OR, and NOT (defined below) and the boolean values true (1) and false (0).

	(NOT)			(AND)	(OR)
A	-A	A	B	A*B	A+B
0	1	0	0	0	0
1	0	0	1	0	1
		1	0	0	1
		1	1	1	1

Just as you can construct an arithmetic expression tree from an arithmetic expression, you can also construct a logic expression tree from a logic expression. For example, the following logic expression

```
( 1 * 0 ) + ( 1 * - 0 )
```

can be expressed in prefix form as

```
+ * 1 0 * 1 - 0
```

Applying the expression tree construction process described in the overview to this expression produces the following logic expression tree.

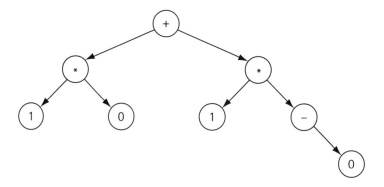

Evaluating this tree yields the boolean value true (1).

Construction of this tree requires processing a unary operator, the boolean operator NOT ('-'). When building a logic expression tree, we will choose to set the right child of any node containing the NOT operator to point to the operand and set the left child to null. Note that you must be careful when performing the remaining operations to avoid traversing these null left children.

Step 1: Add a helper function for `evaluate` that is specialized for `bool` in the file *ExprTree.h* so that this function yields a Boolean value rather than a floating-point number.

Step 2: Create an implementation of the Expression Tree ADT that supports logic expressions consisting of the boolean values true and false ('1' and '0') and the boolean operators AND, OR, and NOT ('*', '+', and '-'). The only change necessary to support the logic expressions is to modify the evaluation function implementation. All other Expression Tree operations work the same on numeric expression trees as logic expression trees. Save your implementation of the evaluate helper in the file *ExprTree.cpp*.

Step 3: Activate Test 1 by changing the value of LAB8_TEST1 from 0 to 1 in the *config.h* file.

Step 4: Compile your expanded implementation of the Expression Tree ADT and the modified test program.

Step 5: Complete Test Plan 8-2 by filling in the expected result for each logic expression. You may wish to include additional logic expressions in this test plan.

Step 6: Execute Test Plan 8-2. If you discover mistakes in your implementation of the Expression Tree ADT, correct them and execute the test plan again.

Having produced a tool that constructs and evaluates logic expression trees, you can use this tool to investigate the use of logic circuits to perform binary arithmetic. Suppose you have two one-bit binary numbers (X and Y). You can add these numbers together to produce a one-bit sum (S) and a one-bit carry (C). The results of one-bit binary addition for all combinations of X and Y are tabulated here.

	X	Y	C	S
X	0	0	0	0
+ Y	0	1	0	1
C S	1	0	0	1
	1	1	1	0

A brief analysis of this table reveals that you can compute the values of outputs S and C from inputs X and Y using the following pair of (prefix) logic expressions.

```
C = *XY       S = +*X-Y*-XY
```

Step 7: Complete Test Plan 8-3 by filling in the expected result for logic expressions C and S.

Step 8: Execute Test Plan 8-3. If you discover mistakes in your implementation of the Expression Tree ADT, correct them and execute the test plan again.

Programming Exercise 2

You no doubt remember the commutative property in mathematics. It guarantees, for instance, that $a + b = b + a$. Swapping the '+' operator's operands results in an expression that has the same value. The commutative property is not true for all operators—a/b is generally not equal to b/a—but the operands of all binary operators can be commuted (swapped). Commuting the operators in an arithmetic expression requires restructuring the nodes in the corresponding expression tree. For example, commuting *every* operator in the expression tree

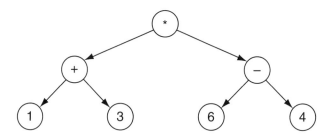

yields the expression tree

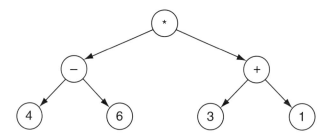

An operation for commuting expression trees is described next.

`void commute ()`

Requirements:
None

Results:
Commutes the operands for every arithmetic operator in the expression tree.

Step 1: Implement this operation and add it to the file *ExprTree.cpp*. A prototype for this operation is included in the declaration of the ExprTree class in the file *ExprTree.h*.

Step 2: Activate the test for the `commute` operation by changing the definition of LAB8_TEST2 in *config.h* from 0 to 1 and recompiling.

Step 3: Prepare Test Plan 8-4 for this operation by including a variety of arithmetic expressions and their expected results after commuting.

Step 4: Execute Test Plan 8-4. If you discover mistakes in your implementation of the commute operation, correct them and execute the test plan again.

Programming Exercise 3

In Programming Exercise 2, you commuted expression trees. Sometimes, a commuted expression tree evaluates to the same value as the original expression tree. This is due to the commutative properties of certain arithmetic operations. In this programming exercise, you determine whether two expression trees are equivalent under the commutative properties. Note: you are not trying to determine whether the trees evaluate to the same value, although equivalent expression trees will evaluate to the same value. In other words, two trees are equivalent if the corresponding nodes are leaves with the same value, if they have the same operator and equivalent subtrees as operands, or if they have the same commutable operator with equivalent, but commuted subtrees as operands.

```
bool isEquivalent ( const ExprTree& other ) const
```

Requirements:
None

Results:
Compares the expression tree to another expression tree for equivalence. If the two trees are equivalent, then returns `true`. Otherwise, returns `false`.

Step 1: Implement this operation and add it to the file *ExprTree.cpp*. A prototype for this operation is included in the declaration of the ExprTree class in the file *ExprTree.h*.

Step 2: Activate the test for the `isEquivalent` operation by changing the definition of LAB8_TEST3 in *config.h* from 0 to 1 and recompiling.

Step 3: Prepare Test Plan 8-5 for this operation by including a variety of arithmetic expressions and their expected results after testing for equivalency.

Step 4: Execute Test Plan 8-5. If you discover mistakes in your implementation of the commute operation, correct them and execute the test plan again.

Analysis Exercise 1

What type of tree traversal (inorder, preorder, or postorder) serves as the basis for your implementation of each of the following Expression Tree ADT operations? Briefly explain why you used a given traversal to implement a particular operation.

Build

Traversal:

Explanation:

Expression

Traversal:

Explanation:

Evaluate

Traversal:

Explanation:

Clear

Traversal:

Explanation:

Analysis Exercise 2

Consider the proposed member functions `writeHelper1` and `writeHelper2` given here:

```
void ExprTree<DataType>:: writeHelper1 ( ExprTreeNode *p ) const {
   if ( p != 0 ){
      writeHelper1(p->left);
      cout << p->dataItem;
      writeHelper1(p->right);
   }
}
```

```
void ExprTree<DataType>:: writeHelper2 ( ExprTreeNode *p ) const {
    if ( p->left != 0 ) writeHelper2(p->left);
    cout << p->dataItem;
    if ( p->right != 0 ) writeHelper2(p->right);
}
```

Let `root` be the pointer to the root node of a nonempty expression tree. Will the following pair of function calls produce the same output?

`writeHelper1(root);` and `writeHelper2(root);`

If not, why not? If so, how do the functions differ and why might this difference be important?

eate
Binary Search
Tree ADT

In this laboratory you will

- create an implementation of the Binary Search Tree ADT using a linked tree structure.

- examine how an index can be used to retrieve records from a database file and construct an indexing program for an accounts database.

- use recursion to perform various tree operations.

- analyze the computational complexity of your implementation of the Binary Search Tree ADT.

ADT Overview

In this laboratory, you examine how a binary tree can be used to represent the hierarchical search process embodied in the binary search algorithm.

The binary search algorithm allows you to efficiently locate a data item in an array provided that each array data item has a unique identifier—called its key—and that the array data items are stored in order based on their keys. Given the following array of keys

Index	0	1	2	3	4	5	6
Key	16	20	31	43	65	72	86

a binary search for the data item with key 31 begins by comparing 31 with the key in the middle of the array, 43. Because 31 is less than 43, the data item with key 31 must lie in the lower half of the array (entries 0-2). The key in the middle of this subarray is 20. Because 31 is greater than 20, the data item with key 31 must lie in the upper half of this subarray (entry 2). This array entry contains the key 31. Thus, the search terminates with success.

Although the comparisons made during a search for a given key depend on the key, the relative order in which comparisons are made is invariant for a given array of data items. For instance, when searching through the previous array, you always compare the key that you are searching for with 43 before you compare it with either 20 or 72. Similarly, you always compare the key with 72 before you compare it with either 65 or 86. The order of comparisons associated with this array is shown here.

Index	0	1	2	3	4	5	6
Key	16	20	31	43	65	72	86
Order compared	3	2	3	1	3	2	3

The hierarchical nature of the comparisons that are performed by the binary search algorithm is reflected in the following tree.

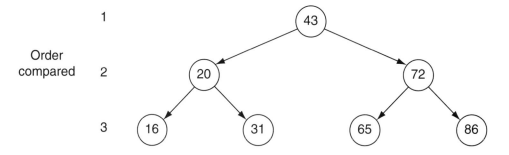

Observe that for each key *K* in this tree, all of the keys in *K*'s left subtree are less than *K* and all of the keys in *K*'s right subtree are greater than *K*. Trees with this property are referred to as binary search trees.

When searching for a key in a binary search tree, you begin at the root node and move downward along a branch until either you find the node containing the key or you reach a leaf node without finding the key. Each move along a branch corresponds to an array subdivision in the binary search algorithm. At each node, you move down to the left if the key you are searching for is less than the key stored in the node, or you move down to the right if the key you are searching for is greater than the key stored in the node.

C++ Concepts Overview

We are repeating the following section on reference pointers in case you did not read Lab 8.

Reference pointers: Pointers and references do not have to be mutually exclusive choices. We can have a reference to a pointer, which can be useful as a parameter to a function. By making a parameter a reference, all changes to the formal parameter are reflected in the actual parameter. This enables creating a parameter that points to an element, but that may point to a different element by the end of a function call.

Binary Search Tree ADT

Data Items

The data items in a binary search tree are of generic type DataType. Each data item has a key (of generic type KeyType) that uniquely identifies the data item. Data items usually include additional data. The data items must provide a function called `getKey` that returns a data item's key. Any type used for KeyType must support the six basic relational operators.

Structure

The data items form a binary tree. For each data item D in the tree, all the data items in D's left subtree have keys that are less than D's key and all the data items in D's right subtree have keys that are greater than D's key.

Operations

`BSTree ()`

Requirements:
None

Results:
Default constructor. Creates an empty binary search tree.

`BSTree ( const BSTree<DataType,KeyType>& other )`

Requirements:
None

Results:
Copy constructor. Initializes the binary search tree to be equivalent to the `other` BSTree object parameter.

```
BSTree& operator= ( const BSTree<DataType,KeyType>& other )
```

Requirements:
None

Results:
Overloaded assignment operator. Sets the binary search tree to be equivalent to the `other` BSTree object parameter and returns a reference to this object.

```
~BSTree ()
```

Requirements:
None

Results:
Destructor. Deallocates (frees) the memory used to store the binary search tree.

```
void insert ( const DataType& newDataItem )
```

Requirements:
None

Results:
Inserts `newDataItem` into the binary search tree. If a data item with the same key as `newDataItem` already exists in the tree, then updates that data item with `newDataItem`.

```
bool retrieve ( const KeyType& searchKey,
                DataType& searchDataItem ) const
```

Requirements:
None

Results:
Searches the binary search tree for the data item with key `searchKey`. If this data item is found, then copies the data item to `searchDataItem` and returns `true`. Otherwise, returns `false` with `searchDataItem` undefined.

```
bool remove ( const KeyType& deleteKey )
```

Requirements:
None

Results:
Deletes the data item with key `deleteKey` from the binary search tree. If this data item is found, then deletes it from the tree and returns `true`. Otherwise, returns `false`.

```
void writeKeys () const
```

Requirements:
None

Results:
Outputs the keys of the data items in the binary search tree. The keys are output in ascending order on one line, separated by spaces.

```
void clear ()
```

Requirements:
None

Results:
Removes all the data items in the binary search tree.

```
bool isEmpty () const
```

Requirements:
None

Results:
Returns `true` if the binary search tree is empty. Otherwise, returns `false`.

```
void showStructure () const
```

Requirements:
None

Results:
Outputs the keys in the binary search tree. The tree is output with its branches oriented from left (root) to right (leaves)—that is, the tree is output rotated counterclockwise ninety degrees from its conventional orientation. If the tree is empty, outputs "Empty tree". Note that this operation is intended for debugging purposes only. It only supports data items with key values that are one of C++'s predefined data types (int, char, and so forth) or other data structures that have overridden ostream `operator<<`.

Implementation Notes

The `isFull` function: The `isFull` function is not included in the ADT. The reason is that it doesn't make much sense to ask whether the tree is full, given that we recommend simply returning `false`. The reason that `isFull` was included in a number of previous ADTs was 1) because it makes sense for an array-based ADT implementation, and 2) we were keeping the linked-list implementation interface compatible with the array-based implementation. Those reasons do not exist with our Binary Search Tree ADT.

The DataType `getKey` member function: The following example (from *test9.cpp*) illustrates how to declare an appropriate data type to be used with the Binary Search

Tree. It meets the Binary Search Tree ADT `DataType` requirements because it has both a key field (`keyField`) and a `getKey` function that returns the value of the key field and that supports the six relational operators.

```
class TestData
{
  public:
    ...
    int getKey () const
        { return keyField; }      // Returns the key
  private:
    ...
    int keyField;                 // Key for the data item
};
int main()
{
    BSTree<TestData,int> testTree;   // Test binary search tree
    ...
```

We are repeating the following sections on helper functions and reference pointers in case you did not read Lab 8.

Helper functions: With functions that are naturally implemented using recursion, it is useful to have a separate function that provides a public interface to the class. That function then calls a private "helper" function with a set of appropriate parameters. The helper function performs the recursive work, while the public interface function ensures that the recursive process gets started correctly and any return value is sent back to the caller.

Reference pointers: To define a parameter that is a reference to a pointer, you simply use both `&` and `*` in the data type specification for the parameter. For example, the following code declares the helper function (`buildHelper`) for the `build` function. The function takes a reference to a pointer to an expression tree node so that if a new node should be added to the tree, it can be allocated and added by simply assigning the newly allocated node to the `node` parameter.

```
template<typename DataType>
void ExprTree<DataType>::buildHelper(ExprTreeNode*& node) {
    . . .
}
```

Note: the order of the `*` and `&` operators is significant. "`*&`" means a reference to a pointer, but "`&*`" means a pointer to a reference, which is nonsense to the compiler.

Step 1: Implement the operations in Binary Search Tree ADT using a linked tree structure. As with the linear linked structures you developed in prior laboratories, your implementation of the linked tree structure uses a pair of classes: one for the nodes in the tree (`BSTreeNode`) and one for the overall tree structure (`BSTree`). Each node in the tree should contain a data item (`dataItem`) and a pair of pointers to the node's children (`left` and `right`). Your implementation should also maintain a pointer to the tree's root node (`root`). Base your implementation on the declarations from the file *BSTree.hs.* An implementation of the `showStructure` operation is given in the file *show9.cpp.*

Step 2: The declaration of the BSTree class in the file *BSTree.hs* does not include prototypes for the recursive private helper functions needed by your implementation of the Binary Search Tree ADT. Add these prototypes and save the resulting BSTree class declaration in the file *BSTree.h*.

Step 3: Save your implementation of the Binary Search Tree ADT in the file *BSTree.cpp*. Be sure to document your code.

Compilation Directions

Step 1: Compile the test program in the file *test9.cpp*.

Testing

The test program in the file *test9.cpp* allows you to interactively test your implementation of the Binary Search Tree ADT using the following commands.

Command	Action
+key	Insert (or update) the data item with the specified key.
?key	Retrieve the data item with the specified key and output it.
-key	Delete the data item with the specified key.
K	Output the keys in ascending order.
E	Report whether the tree is empty.
C	Clear the tree.
Q	Quit the test program.

Step 1: Complete Test Plan 9-1 for your implementation of the Binary Search Tree ADT. Your test plan should cover trees of various shapes and sizes, including empty, single-branch, and single-data item trees.

Step 2: Execute Test Plan 9-1. If you discover mistakes in your implementation, correct them and execute your test plan again.

Programming Exercise 1

A database is a collection of related pieces of information that is organized for easy retrieval. The set of accounts records shown below (from *accounts.dat*), for instance, form an accounts database.

Record #	Account ID	First name	Last name	Balance
0	6274	James	Johnson	415.56
1	2843	Marcus	Wilson	9217.23
2	4892	Maureen	Albright	51462.56
3	8837	Debra	Douglas	27.26
4	1892	Mary	Smith	918.26
5	9523	Bruce	Gold	719.32
6	3165	John	Carlson	1496.24
7	3924	Simon	Becker	386.85
8	6023	John	Edgar	9.65
9	5290	George	Truman	16110.68
10	8529	Ellen	Fairchild	86.77
11	1144	Donald	Williams	4114.26

Each record in the accounts database is assigned a record number based on that record's relative position within the database file. You could use a record number to retrieve a record directly, much as you can use an array index to reference an array data item directly. Record numbers are assigned by the database file mechanism and are not part of the account information. As a result, they are not meaningful to database users. These users require a different record retrieval mechanism, one that is based on an account ID (the key for the database) rather than a record number.

Retrievals based on account ID require an index that associates each account ID with the corresponding record number. You can implement this index using a binary search tree in which each data item contains the two fields: an account ID (the key) and a record number.

```
struct IndexEntry
{
    int acctID;              // (Key) Account identifier
    long recNum;             // Record number

    int getKey () const
        { return acctID; }   // Return key field
};

BSTree<IndexEntry,int> index;        // Database index
```

You build the index by reading through the database account-by-account, inserting successive (account ID, record number) pairs into the tree as you progress through the file. The following index tree, for instance, was produced by inserting account records 0-5 (shown previously) into an (initially) empty tree.

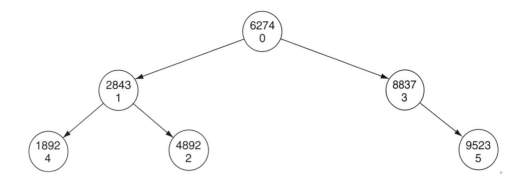

Given an account ID, retrieval of the corresponding account record is a two-step process. First, you retrieve the data item from the index tree that has the specified account ID. Then, using the record number stored in the index data item, you read the corresponding account record from the database file. The result is an efficient retrieval process that is based on account ID.

Step 1: Using the program shell given in the file *database.cs* as a basis, create a program that builds an index tree for the accounts database in the file *accounts.dat*. Save the program in *database.cpp*. Once the index is built, your program should

- output the account IDs in ascending order, and
- read an account ID from the keyboard and output the corresponding account record.

Step 2: Compile *database.cpp*.

Step 3: Fill in Test Plan 9-2 using the accounts database in the text file *accounts.dat*. A copy of this database was given previously. Try to retrieve several account IDs, including account IDs that do *not* occur in the database.

Step 4: Execute Test Plan 9-2. If you discover mistakes in your implementation of the Binary Search Tree ADT, correct them and execute the test plan again.

Programming Exercise 2

It can be useful to know how many nodes a binary search tree contains. The following new Binary Search Tree ADT operation adds the capability to interrogate a tree to find out how many data items it contains.

```
int getCount () const
```

Requirements:
None

Results:
Returns the count of the number of data items in the binary search tree.

Binary search trees containing the same data items can vary widely in shape depending on the order in which the data items were inserted into the trees. One measurement of a tree's shape is its height—that is, the number of nodes on the longest path from the root node to any leaf node. This statistic is significant because the amount of time that it can take to search for a data item in a binary search tree is a function of the height of the tree.

You can compute the height of a binary search tree using a postorder traversal and the following recursive definition of height for a tree rooted at a given node *p*.

$$height(p)=\begin{cases}0 & \text{if } p \text{ is null } (base\ case)\\ \max(height(p\rightarrow\text{left}), height(p\rightarrow\text{right}))+1 & \text{if } p \text{ is not null } (recursive\ step)\end{cases}$$

```
int getHeight () const
```

Requirements:
None

Results:
Returns the height of the binary search tree.

Step 1: Implement these two operations (the two member functions and their helper functions) and add them to the file *BSTree.cpp*. Prototypes for `getCount` and `getHeight` are included in the declaration of the BSTree class in the file *BSTree.h*, but you will need to add prototypes for the helper functions.

Step 2: Activate Test 1 to test `getCount` by changing the definition of LAB9_TEST1 in *config.h* from 0 to 1 and recompiling.

Step 3: Prepare Test Plan 9-3 for this operation by including a variety of different binary search trees and the expected results of calling `getCount`.

Step 4: Execute Test Plan 9-3. If you discover mistakes in your implementation of the `getCount` operation, correct them and execute the test plan again.

Step 5: Activate Test 2 to test `getHeight` by changing the definition of LAB9_TEST2 in *config.h* from 0 to 1 and recompiling.

Step 6: Prepare Test Plan 9-4 for this operation by including a variety of different binary search trees and the expected results of calling `getHeight`.

Step 7: Execute Test Plan 9-4. If you discover mistakes in your implementation of the `getHeight` operation, correct them and execute the test plan again.

Programming Exercise 3

You have created operations that retrieve a single data item from a binary search tree and output all the keys in a tree. The following operation outputs only keys that are less than the specified value.

```
void writeLessThan ( const KeyType& searchKey ) const
```

Requirements:
None

Results:
Outputs all keys in a binary search tree that are less than `searchKey`. The keys are output in ascending order using the same format as `writeKeys`. Note that `searchKey` need not be a key in the tree.

You could implement this operation using an inorder traversal of the entire tree in which you compare each key with `searchKey` and output those that are less than `searchKey`. Although successful, this approach is inefficient. It searches subtrees that you know cannot possibly contain keys that are less than `searchKey`.

Suppose you are given a `searchKey` value of 37 and the following binary search tree.

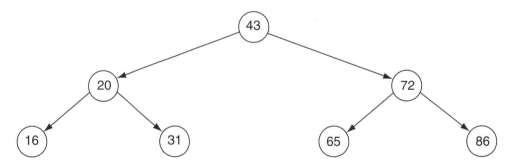

Because the root node contains the key 43, you can determine immediately that you do not need to search the root node's right subtree for keys that are less than 37. Similarly, if the value of `searchKey` were 67, then you would need to search the root node's right subtree but would not need to search the right subtree of the node whose key is 72. Your implementation of the `writeLessThan` operation should use this idea to limit the portion of the tree that must be searched.

Step 1: Implement this operation and add it to *BSTree.cpp*. A prototype for this operation is included in the declaration of the BSTree class in the file *BSTree.h.*

Step 2: Activate Test 3 to test `writeLessThan` by changing the definition of LAB9_TEST3 in *config.h* from 0 to 1 and recompiling.

Step 3: Prepare Test Plan 9-5 for this operation by including a variety of binary search trees and values for searchKey, including values of searchKey that do *not* occur in a particular tree. Be sure to include test cases that limit searches to the left subtree of the root node, the left subtree and part of the right subtree of the root node, the leftmost branch in the tree, and the entire tree.

Step 4: Execute Test Plan 9-5. If you discover mistakes in your implementation of the `writeLessThan` operation, correct them and execute the test plan again.

Analysis Exercise 1

What are the heights of the shortest and tallest binary search trees that can be constructed from a set of N distinct keys? Give examples that illustrate your answer.

Analysis Exercise 2

Given the shortest possible binary search tree containing N distinct keys, develop worst-case, order-of-magnitude estimates of the execution time of the following Binary Search Tree ADT operations. Briefly explain your reasoning behind each of your estimates.

retrieve	O( )
Explanation:	

insert	O( )
Explanation:	

remove	O( )
Explanation:	

writeKeys	O( )
Explanation:	

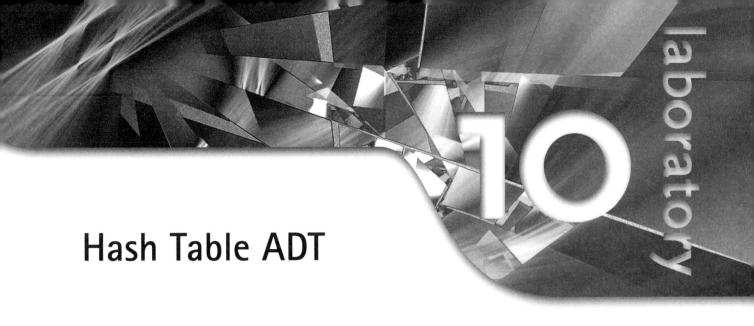

Hash Table ADT

In this laboratory you

- implement the Hash Table ADT using an array of binary search trees representation.

- implement a perfect hash.

- analyze the uniformity of the key distribution using standard deviation analysis.

- analyze the computational complexity of your implementation of the Hash Table ADT.

ADT Overview

The data structures that you have implemented up to this point are all useful and widely used. However, their average performance for insertion and retrieval is generally O(N), or at best O($\log_2 N$). As N becomes large–*large* is a relative term, depending on current hardware configuration and performance, data record size and a number of other factors, but let's say hundreds of thousands or millions of records– O(N) becomes a poor choice. Even O($\log_2 N$) performance can be unacceptable when handling many simultaneous queries or processing large reports. How does searching, inserting, and retrieving in O(1) sound? That is the possibility that the Hash Table ADT tries to offer. Hash tables are among the fastest data structures for most operations and come closest to offering O(1) performance. Consequently, a hash table is the preferred data structure in many contexts. For instance, online library catalogs are typically implemented using hash tables.

The goal of the ideal hash table is to come up with a unique mapping of each key onto a specific location in an array. The mapping of the key to a specific location in an array is handled by the hash operation. A hash operation will accept the key as input and return an integer that is used as an index into the hash table.

How does this work? The simplest case occurs when the key is an integer. Then the hash function could simply return an integer. For instance, given the key 3, the hash function would return the index value 3 to place the record in the hash table position 3. The key 1 would be used to place the record in hash table position 1.

Index	0	1	2	3	4	5	6
Key		1		3			

But what about a key value of 9? The array used to implement the hash table does not have a valid position 9, so some set of operations must be performed on the key in order to map it to an index value that is a valid index for the array. A simple solution to this problem is to perform a modulus operation with the table size on the key value. Using the example of 9 for the table of size 7 above, the hash function would calculate 9 modulus 7 to produce an index value of 2.

Unfortunately, it is easy for the hash calculation to generate the same index value for more than one key. This is called a collision. Using a key of 10 in the example above, the hash calculation would produce 3–calculated as 10 modulus 7 (`10%7` in C++). But position 3 already has a key associated with it–the key 3. There are a number of methods that can be used to resolve the collision. The one we use is called chaining. When using chaining, all the keys that generate a particular index are connected to that array position in a chain–or another data structure. One way to implement chaining is by associating a binary search tree with each table entry. Using this approach, position 0 in the hash table would have a binary search tree of all data items for which the hash operation produces an index of 0, position 1 would have a binary search tree of all data items associated with index 1, and so on through index 6. The key values 1, 3, 7, 8, 10, and 13 would produce the following chains associated with the indexes 0, 1, 3, and 6.

Index	0	1	2	3	4	5	6
Key	7	1		3			13
		8		10			

Generating an index for other key types is more complicated than for integers. For instance, if the key for a record is a string, the string could be mapped to an integer by adding up the ASCII values of each of the characters in the string. Given a last name of "smith", the function could calculate a value of 115 ('s') + 109 ('m') + 105 ('i') + 116 ('t') + 104 ('h') = 549. Real numbers can be mapped to integers by simply truncating the non-integer part.

Note that these are simple examples of hash operations intended as an introduction to the hash tables. A more detailed explanation would go into great detail about how to take a key and move the bits around to produce a high quality key that will ensure a fairly uniform distribution of data items throughout the table. See Programming Exercise 3 for more detail.

C++ Concepts Overview

Unsigned int: Programming languages that support integers typically have two types of integer, signed and unsigned. A signed integer is one that supports negative numbers as well as positive numbers. An unsigned integer only supports zero and positive numbers. It is useful because for a given number of bits, it can represent twice as large a positive number as is possible with a signed integer. And there are situations when the result of a computation must not be negative.

Structs vs. classes in C++: The example implementation (given in the implementation section) uses a `struct` with static methods, etc. for DataType. The essential difference between a class and a struct in C++ is that in a struct everything is by default public, but everything is by default private in a class.

Hash Table ADT

Data items

The data items in a hash table are of generic type DataType. Each data item has a key of the generic type KeyType that uniquely identifies the data item. Data items usually include additional data. Type DataType must provide a function called `getKey` that returns a data item's key and a static method called `hash` that returns an `unsigned int` and receives a `const` reference to a KeyType as a parameter.

Structure

This hash table ADT is an array of binary search trees. The placement of the data items in a particular binary search tree is determined by the index calculated using the DataType's static method named `hash`. The placement within a particular binary search tree is determined by the chronological order in which the data items are inserted into the list—the earliest insertion takes place at the root of the binary search tree, the most recent as a leaf of the binary search tree. The ordering within a particular binary search tree is *not* a function of the data contained in the hash table data items. You interact with each binary search tree by using the standard binary search tree operations.

Operations

```
HashTable ( int initTableSize )
```

Requirements:
None

Results:
Constructor. Creates the empty hash table.

```
HashTable ( const HashTable& other )
```

Requirements:
None

Results:
Copy constructor. Initializes the hash table to be equivalent to the HashTable object parameter `other`.

```
HashTable& operator= ( const HashTable& other )
```

Requirements:
None

Results:
Overloaded assignment operator. Sets the hash table to be equivalent to the `other` HashTable object parameter and returns a reference to this object.

```
~HashTable ()
```

Requirements:
None

Results:
Destructor. Deallocates (frees) the memory used to store a hash table.

```
void insert ( const DataType& newDataItem )
```

Requirements:
None

Results:
Inserts `newDataItem` into the appropriate binary search tree. If a data item with the same key as `newDataItem` already exists in the binary search tree, then updates that data item with `newDataItem`. Otherwise, it inserts it in the binary search tree.

```
bool remove ( const KeyType& deleteKey )
```

Requirements:
None

Results:
Searches the hash table for the data item with the key `deleteKey`. If the data item is found, then removes the data item and returns `true`. Otherwise, returns `false`.

```
bool retrieve ( const KeyType& searchKey,
                DataType& returnItem ) const
```

Requirements:
None

Results:
Searches the hash table for the data item with key `searchKey`. If the data item is found, then copies the data item to `returnItem` and returns `true`. Otherwise, returns `false` with `returnItem` undefined.

```
void clear ()
```

Requirements:
None

Results:
Removes all data items in the hash table.

```
bool isEmpty () const
```

Requirements:
None

Results:
Returns `true` if the hash table is empty. Otherwise, returns `false`.

```
void showStructure () const
```

Requirements:
None

Results:
Outputs the data items in the hash table. If the hash table is empty, outputs "Empty hash table". Note that this operation is intended for testing/debugging purposes only. It only supports data items with key values that are one of C++'s predefined data types (int, char, and so forth) or other data structures that have overridden ostream `operator<<`.

Implementation Notes

You can implement a hash table in many ways. We have chosen to implement the hash table using chaining to resolve collisions. The binary search tree ADT provides a simple way of dealing with a chain of data items and is an opportunity to use one of your ADTs to implement another ADT. Your instructor may choose to let you use one of the STL containers instead.

Step 1: Implement the operations in the Hash Table ADT using an array of binary search trees to store the hash table data items. You need to store the number of hash table slots (`tableSize`) and the actual hash table itself (`dataTable`). Base your implementation on the file *HashTable.h*. An implementation of the showStructure operation is given in the file *show10.cpp*. If you are using an STL container, modify the showStructure operation to work with that STL container.

Step 2: Save your implementation of the Hash Table ADT in the file *HashTable.cpp*. Be sure to document your code.

The following program was adapted from the Lab 4 (Ordered List ADT) implementation notes. It reads in account numbers and balances for a set of accounts. It then tries retrieving records using the account numbers as the keys. The primary change is that the Account struct needs to have a hash static method added to be usable with the hash table. We also removed the code outputting the accounts in ascending order based on their account numbers because an ordered traversal of the hash table is not something supported by this Hash Table ADT.

```cpp
// lab10-example1.cpp
#include <iostream>
#include <cmath>
#include "HashTable.cpp"
using namespace std;
struct Account
{
    int acctNum;                // (Key) Account number
    float balance;             // Account balance
    int getKey () const { return acctNum; }
    static unsigned int hash(const int& key) { return abs( key ); }
};


int main()
{
    HashTbl<Account,int> accounts(11);    // List of accounts
    Account acct;                          // A single account
    int searchKey;                         // An account key
    // Read in information on a set of accounts.
    cout << endl << "Enter account information (num balance) for 5 accounts: "
        << endl;
    for ( int i = 0; i < 5; i++ )
    {
        cin >> acct.acctNum >> acct.balance;
        accounts.insert(acct);
    }
    // Checks for accounts and prints records if found
    cout << endl;
    cout << "Enter account number (<EOF> to end): ";
    while ( cin >> searchKey )
    {
        if ( accounts.retrieve(searchKey,acct) )
            cout << acct.acctNum << " " << acct.balance << endl;
        else
            cout << "Account " << searchKey << " not found." << endl;
    }
}
```

Compilation Directions

Step 1: Compile the test program in the file *test10.cpp*.

Testing

The test program in the file *test10.cpp* allows you to interactively test your implementation of the Hash Table ADT using the following commands.

Command	Action
+key	Insert (or update) data item with key value *key*.
-key	Remove the data item with the key value *key*.
?key	Retrieve the item with the specified key and output it.
E	Report whether the table is empty.
C	Clear the table.
Q	Quit the test program.

Step 1: Prepare Test Plan 10-1 for your implementation of the Hash Table ADT. Your test plan should cover the application of each operation.

Step 2: Execute Test Plan 10-1. If you discover mistakes in your implementation, correct them and execute your test plan again.

Programming Exercise 1

One possible use for a hash table is to store computer user login usernames and passwords. Your program should load username/password sets from the file *password.dat* and insert them into the hash table until end of file is reached on *password.dat*. There is one username/password set (separated by a tab) per line as shown in the following example.

```
jack        broken.crown
jill        tumblin'down
mary        contrary
bopeep      sheep!lost
```

Your program should present a login prompt, read one username, present a password prompt, read the password, and then print either "Authentication successful" or "Authentication failure" as shown in the following examples.

Login: jack

Password: broken.crown

Authentication successful

Login: jill

Password: tumblingdown

Authentication failure

This authentication loop is to be repeated until the end of input data—EOF—is reached on the console input stream (cin).

Step 1: Prepare Test Plan 10-2 that specifies how you will verify that your program works correctly.

Step 2: Create a program that will read in the usernames and passwords from *password.dat* and then allow the user to try authenticating usernames and passwords as shown as long as the user enters more data. Store your program in the file *login.cpp*.

Create an appropriate class to hold the username/password pairs in the hash table.

Step 3: Compile *login.cpp* and execute Test Plan 10-2. If you discover mistakes, correct them and execute your test plan again.

Programming Exercise 2

A hash table insertion or retrieval with no collisions has O(1) operation. Collisions reduce the O(1) behavior to something less desirable. There are two ways to reduce collisions:

- Increase the size of the table. As the table size increases, the statistical probability of collisions for unique keys decreases. The problem with arbitrarily increasing the table size is that the amount of physical memory is finite and declaring a wildly large table in the hope of reducing collisions wastes memory.
- Enhance the quality of the `hash` static method so that it produces fewer collisions. Ideally, unique keys have unique indexes into the hash table and no collisions. This situation is called a perfect hash. The problem with generating perfect hashes is that the hash function must be very carefully crafted to avoid collisions and becomes progressively harder with more keys.

A minimal perfect hash is a hash table with the following two properties:

- The minimal property—the memory allocated to store the keywords is exactly large enough to hold the needed number of keys and no more. For *n* keys, there are exactly *n* table entries.
- The perfect property—locating a table entry requires at most one key comparison. There are no collisions. Consequently, no collision resolution is required.

Software developers like minimal perfect hash tables for specific sets of strings because of the performance boost. For instance, it is very helpful if a C++ compiler can perform an O(1) lookup on a string to determine whether it is a C++ reserved word.

Step 1: Develop a `hash` static method implementation that will produce a minimal perfect hash for the following seven C++ reserved words: `double`, `else`, `if`, `return`, `switch`, `void`, and `while`.

Use the following class to hold the strings.

```
class Identifier {
    string ident;
  public:
    void setKey(string newIdent)
    { ident = newIdent; }
    string getKey() const
          { return ident; }
    static unsigned int hash( const string& key )
          { return . . . }
};
```

Step 2: Prepare Test Plan 10-3 that specifies how you will validate that your `hash` static method works correctly to generate a minimal perfect hash table.

Step 3: Implement a test program using the previous class to demonstrate that you have indeed developed a minimal perfect hash for the given seven C++ identifiers. Save your program in the file *perfect.cpp*. Use the provided `showStructure` function to display the hash table after all the data has been entered.

Step 4: Execute Test Plan 10-3. If you discover mistakes in your implementation of the `hash` static method, correct them and execute your test plan again.

Programming Exercise 3

Performance of hash tables depends on how uniformly the keys are distributed among the table entries. In the ideal situation—a minimal perfect hash, see Programming Exercise 2—there is exactly one data item per hash table entry. Unfortunately, minimal perfect hashes become progressively more difficult to generate as the number of data items increases. In the worst possible key distribution scenario, all the data items would be chained off one hash table entry and all the other table entries would be empty. This is essentially a binary search tree and the performance benefits of the hash table are lost. Rather than trying to develop a perfect hash, developers usually build a hash function that will attempt to distribute the keys uniformly across all the table entries. Each table entry will have the same—or almost the same—number of keys associated with it.

Suppose that you have developed a hash function that you believe does a satisfactory job of distributing keys over the table. A good question to ask is "How uniform a distribution is the hash function achieving?" The formal mathematical answers are beyond the scope of this lab text. However, one simple way of calculating this is to calculate the standard deviation of the number of data items associated with each table entry. The standard deviation number does not claim to answer whether or not a particular hash implementation is good or bad, but it can be used as a rough comparison among hash functions used with the same table size and set of keys. The smaller the number obtained, the closer the hash function comes to providing a uniform distribution.

The formula to calculate the standard deviation, s, is

$$s = \sqrt{\frac{\sum\left(x_i - \bar{x}\right)^2}{n-1}}$$

where $\bar{x}$ represents the average number of keys chained off each table location, x_i represents the number of keys chained at table location i, and n represents the number of array entries in the table.

Standard deviation is calculated as follows:

1. Calculate and save the average—or mean—number of data items per table entry.
2. For each table entry, calculate and save *(number of items – mean number of items)²*.
3. Compute the sum of all the values calculated in Step 2.
4. Divide the result from Step 3 by $n-1$, where n is the number of hash table entries.
5. Calculate the square root of the result obtained in Step 4. This is the standard deviation.

Implement the following new Hash Table ADT operation—`standardDeviation`—that will calculate the standard deviation for key distribution in the hash table.

```
double standardDeviation ( ) const
```

Requirements:
None

Results:
Computes the standard deviation for key distribution in the hash table and returns the result.

Step 1: Implement this operation and add it to the file *HashTable.cpp*. A prototype for this operation is included in the declaration of the Hash Table class in the file *HashTable.h*.

Step 2: The program in the file *test10std.cpp* will read data into a hash table and test your `standardDeviation` operation. Uncomment hash algorithm 1 in the struct `Data`, complete the expected distribution quality, compile and run the test program, and record the results in test results Table 10-4. Comment out hash algorithm 1.

Step 3: Repeat Step 2 for each of the five hash algorithms. For algorithms 4 and 5, you are expected to design your own algorithms, ones that you hope will result in good distributions.

Step 4: Discuss the results with your lab instructor.

Analysis Exercise 1

Given a hash table of size *T*, containing *N* data items, develop worst-case, order-of-magnitude estimates of the execution time of the following Hash Table ADT operations, assuming they are implemented using singly-linked lists for the chained data items and a reasonably uniform distribution of data item keys. Briefly explain your reasoning behind each estimate.

> insert   O(   )
>
> Explanation:

> retrieve   O(   )
>
> Explanation:

What if the chaining is implemented using a binary search tree instead of a singly-linked list? Using the same assumptions as before, develop worst-case, order-of-magnitude estimates of the execution time of the following Hash Table ADT operations. Briefly explain your reasoning behind each estimate.

> insert   O(   )
>
> Explanation:

> retrieve   O(   )
>
> Explanation:

Analysis Exercise 2

Part A

For some large number of data items—e.g., *N*=1,000,000—would you rather use a binary search tree or a hash table for performing data retrieval? Explain your reasoning.

Part B

Assuming the same number of data items given in Part A, would the binary search tree or the hash table be most memory efficient? Explain your assumptions and your reasoning.

Part C

If you needed to select either the binary search tree or the hash table as the general purpose best data structure, which would you choose? Under what circumstances would you choose the other data structure as preferable? Explain your reasoning.

Heap ADT

In this laboratory you

■ create an implementation of the Heap ADT using an array representation of a tree.

■ use inheritance to derive a priority queue class from your heap class and develop a simulation of an operating system's task scheduler using a priority queue.

■ create a heap sort function based on the heap construction techniques used in your implementation of the Heap ADT.

■ analyze where data items with various priorities are located in a heap.

ADT Overview

Linked structures are not the only way in which you can represent trees. If you take the binary tree shown below and copy its contents into an array in level order, you produce the following array.

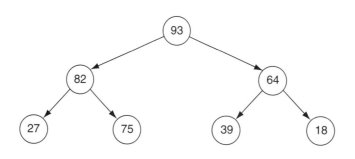

Index	Entry
0	93
1	82
2	64
3	27
4	75
5	39
6	18

Examining the relationship between positions in the tree and entries in the array, you see that if a data item is stored in entry N in the array, then the data item's left child is stored in entry $2N+1$, its right child is stored in entry $2N+2$, and its parent is stored in entry $(N-1)$ mod 2. These mappings make it easy to move through the tree stepping from parent to child (or vice versa).

You could use these mappings to support an array-based implementation of the Binary Search Tree ADT. However, the result would be a tree representation in which large areas of the array are left unused (as indicated by the "–" character in the array below).

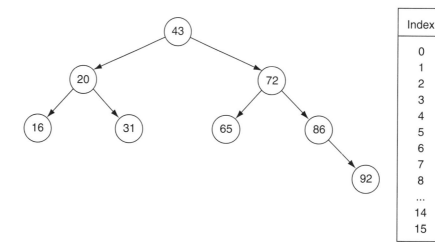

Index	Entry
0	43
1	20
2	72
3	16
4	31
5	65
6	86
7	–
8	–
...	...
14	–
15	92

In this laboratory, you focus on a different type of tree called a heap. A heap is a binary tree that meets the following conditions.

- The tree is complete. That is, every level in the tree is full, except possibly the bottom level. If the bottom level is not full, then all the missing data items occur on the right.
- Each data item in the tree has a corresponding priority value. For each data item E, all of E's descendants have priorities that are less than E's priority. Note that priorities are *not* required to be unique.

The first tree shown on the first page of this laboratory is a heap, as is the tree shown below.

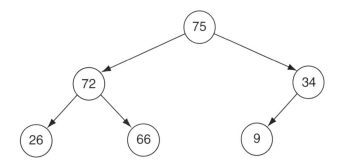

The fact that the tree is complete means that a heap can be stored in level order in an array without introducing gaps (unused areas) in the middle. The result is a compact representation in which you can easily move up and down the branches in a heap.

Clearly, the relationship between the priorities of the various data items in a heap is not strong enough to support an efficient search process. Because the relationship is simple, however, you can quickly restructure a heap after removing the highest priority (root) data item or after inserting a new data item. As a result, you can rapidly process the data items in a heap in descending order based on priority. This property combined with the compact array representation makes a heap an ideal representation for a priority queue (Programming Exercise 1) and forms the basis for an efficient sorting algorithm called heap sort (Programming Exercise 2).

C++ Concepts Overview

Default template types: Just as C++ allows you to specify the default value for a parameter to a function, so it also allows you to specify the default type for a parameter to a template. This allows the programmer to use sensible defaults at class instantiation most of the time.

Template template parameters: Sometimes it is beneficial to pass a templated class (*C*) parameter to another templated class (*T*). Of course, the first class (*C*) must have types passed to it to be meaningful; this results in template parameters with template parameters. See implementation notes for a concrete example.

Overloading the function operator: The function operator, '( )', can be overloaded, just like any other operator. This allows us to treat a class as if it were a function. A practical implication is that you can pass classes to templated classes and override functionality within the templated class. For instance, if you wished to compare two values, but wished to maintain flexibility in the comparison operation, this would let you specify which comparison operation to use for the instantiated class.

Heap ADT

Data Items

The data items in a heap are of generic type DataType. Each data item has a priority that is used to determine the relative position of the data item within the heap. Data items usually include additional data. Note that priorities are *not* required to be unique—it is quite likely that several data items have the same priority. Objects of type DataType must support the six basic relational operators, as well as a function called `getPriority` that returns a data item's priority.

Structure

The data items form a complete binary tree. For each data item E in the tree, all of E's descendants have priorities that are less than or equal to E's priority.

Operations

`Heap ( int maxNumber = MAX_HEAP_SIZE )`

Requirements:
None

Results:
Constructor. Creates an empty heap. Allocates enough memory for a heap containing `maxNumber` data items.

`Heap ( const Heap& other )`

Requirements:
None

Results:
Copy constructor. Initializes the object to be an equivalent copy of `other`.

`Heap& operator = ( const Heap& other )`

Requirements:
None

Results:
Overloaded assignment operator. Sets the heap to be equivalent to the `other` Heap and returns a reference to this object.

`~Heap ( )`

Requirements:
None

Results:
Destructor. Deallocates (frees) the memory used to store the heap.

[handwritten margin notes:] Node 0 / left $2j+1$ / right $2j+2$ / parent $j-1/2$

```
void insert ( const DataType& newDataItem ) throw ( logic_error )
```

Requirements:
Heap is not full.

Results:
Inserts `newDataItem` into the heap. Inserts this data item as the bottom rightmost data item in the heap and moves it upward until the properties that define a heap are restored.

```
DataType remove () throw ( logic_error )
```

Requirements:
Heap is not empty.

Results:
Removes the data item with the highest priority (the root) from the heap and returns it. Replaces the root data item with the bottom rightmost data item and moves this data item downward until the properties that define a heap are restored.

```
void clear ()
```

Requirements:
None

Results:
Removes all the data items in the heap.

```
bool isEmpty () const
```

Requirements:
None

Results:
Returns `true` if the heap is empty. Otherwise, returns `false`.

```
bool isFull () const
```

Requirements:
None

Results:
Returns `true` if the heap is full. Otherwise, returns `false`.

```
void showStructure () const
```

Requirements:
None

Results:
Outputs the priorities of the data items in the heap in both array and tree form. The tree is output with its branches oriented from left (root) to right (leaves)—that is, the tree is output rotated counterclockwise ninety degrees from its conventional orientation. If the heap is empty, outputs "Empty heap". Note that this operation is intended for testing/debugging purposes only.

Implementation Notes

Default template types: The syntax for specifying default template data types is to follow the template named type by '=' and the default type. This should be done in the template declaration, e.g., *Heap.h*—not in the definition, e.g., *Heap.cpp*. The following code illustrates how the Heap class uses default template types.

```
template < typename DataType, typename KeyType=int,
           typename Comparator=Less<KeyType> >
class Heap { ... };
```

Template template parameters: Note the `Less` parameter to the template above. It is an example of a template template parameter since it takes `KeyType` as a parameter while `KeyType` is a parameter to `Heap` so `KeyType` is not an actual type, but a template for the type that is passed to `Heap`. `Comparator` is receiving a template for its template parameter! By having `Comparator` use `KeyType`, we ensure it is comparing the same values that the `Heap` is using for keys. We now have a generic function that will work with any data type for our heap as long as the < operator is defined for the key field.

Overloading the function operator: Like any other overloaded operator, we create the overloaded function operator by creating a new function named "`operator()`". The new idea is how to call the overloaded operator. If class *O* has an overloaded function operator, we can create an object *obj* of type *O*. We then call the function operator by treating *obj* as if it were a function and using it like any other function. The following code shows how the Heap uses the Comparator class in this manner.

```
// create an object called compare
Comparator compare;
...
// treat compare object as a function
if (compare(a.getPriority(), b.getPriority()))
    // place a before b
```

Step 1: Implement the operations in Heap ADT using an array representation of a heap. Heaps can be different sizes, therefore you need to store the maximum number of data items the heap can hold (`maxSize`) and the actual number of data items in the heap (`size`), along with the heap data items themselves (`dataItems`). Base your implementation on the following declarations from the file *Heap.h*. An implementation of the `showStructure` operation is given in the file *show11.cpp*.

Step 2: Save your implementation of the Heap ADT in the file *Heap.cpp*. Be sure to document your code.

Compilation Directions

Compile *test11.cpp*.

Testing

The test program in the file *test11.cpp* allows you to interactively test your implementation of the Heap ADT using the following commands.

Command	Action
+pty	Insert a data item with the specified priority.
-	Remove the data item with the highest priority from the heap and output it.
E	Report whether the heap is empty.
F	Report whether the heap is full.
C	Clear the heap.
Q	Quit the test program.

Step 1: Download the online test plans for Lab 11.

Step 2: Prepare Test Plan 11-1 for your implementation of the Heap ADT. Your test plan should cover heaps of various sizes, including empty, full, and single-data item heaps.

Step 3: Execute your test plan. If you discover mistakes in your implementation, correct them and execute your test plan again.

Programming Exercise 1

A priority queue is a linear data structure in which the data items are maintained in descending order based on priority. You can only access the data item at the front of the queue—that is, the data item with the highest priority—and examining this data item entails removing (dequeuing) it from the queue.

Priority Queue ADT

Data Items

The data items in a priority queue are of generic type DataType. Each data item has a priority that is used to determine the relative position of the data item within the queue. Data items usually include additional data. Objects of type DataType must support the six basic relational operators, as well as a function called `getPriority` that returns the data item's priority.

Structure

The queue data items are stored in descending order based on priority.

Operations

```
PriorityQueue ( int maxNumber = MAX_QUEUE_SIZE )
```

Requirements:
None

Results:
Constructor. Creates an empty priority queue. Allocates enough memory for a queue containing `maxNumber` data items.

```
PriorityQueue ( const Heap& other )
```

Requirements:
None

Results:
Copy constructor. Initializes the object to be an equivalent copy of `other`.

```
PriorityQueue& operator = ( const PriorityQueue& other )
```

Requirements:
None

Results:
Overloaded assignment operator. Sets the priority queue to be equivalent to the `other` priority queue and returns a reference to this object.

```
~PriorityQueue ()
```

Requirements:
None

Results:
Destructor. Deallocates (frees) the memory used to store the priority queue.

```
void enqueue ( const DataType& newDataItem ) throw ( logic_error )
```

Requirements:
Queue is not full.

Results:
Inserts `newDataItem` into the priority queue.

```
DataType dequeue () throw ( logic_error )
```

Requirements:
Queue is not empty.

Results:
Removes the highest priority (front) data item from the priority queue and returns it.

```
void clear ()
```

Requirements:
None

Results:
Removes all the data items in the priority queue.

```
bool isEmpty () const
```

Requirements:
None

Results:
Returns `true` if the priority queue is empty. Otherwise, returns `false`.

```
bool isFull () const
```

Requirements:
None

Results:
Returns `true` if the priority queue is full. Otherwise, returns `false`.

You can easily and efficiently implement a priority queue as a heap by using the Heap ADT `insert` operation to enqueue data items and the `remove` operation to dequeue data items. The declarations from the file *PriorityQueue.h* derive a class called PriorityQueue from the Heap class.

Implementations of the Priority Queue ADT constructor, enqueue, and dequeue operations are given in the file *PriorityQueue.cpp*. These implementations are very short, reflecting the close relationship between the Heap ADT and the Priority Queue ADT. Note that you inherit the remaining operations in the Priority Queue ADT from the Heap class.

Operating systems commonly use priority queues to regulate access to system resources such as printers, memory, disks, software, and so forth. Each time a task requests access to a system resource, the task is placed on the priority queue associated with that resource. When the task is dequeued, it is granted access to the resource to print, store data, and so on.

Suppose you wish to model the flow of tasks through a priority queue having the following properties:

- One task is dequeued every minute (assuming that there is at least one task waiting to be dequeued during that minute).
- From zero to two tasks are enqueued every minute, where there is a 50% chance that no tasks are enqueued, a 25% percent chance that one task is enqueued, and a 25% chance that two tasks are enqueued.
- Each task has a priority value of zero (low) or one (high), where there is an equal chance of a task having either of these values.

You can simulate the flow of tasks through the queue during a time period n minutes long using the following algorithm.

Initialize the queue to empty.

While the simulation is not done

    Increment simulated time by one minute.

    If the queue is not empty, then remove the task at the front of the queue.

    Compute a random integer k between 0 and 3.

    If k is 1, then add one task to the queue.

    If k is 2, then add two tasks.

    Otherwise (if k is 0 or 3), do not add any tasks to the queue.

    Compute the priority of each task by generating a random value of 0 or 1.

Step 1: Using the program shell given in the file *ossim.cs* as a basis, create a program that uses the Priority Queue ADT to implement the task scheduler described above. Your program should output the following information about each task as it is dequeued: the task's priority, when it was enqueued, and how long it waited in the queue.

Step 2: Use your program to simulate the flow of tasks through the priority queue and complete Table 11-2 in the online supplements.

Step 3: Fill in your answers to Questions 1 and 2 on the Programming Exercises 1 worksheet: "Is your priority queue task scheduler unfair—that is, given two tasks T_1 and T_2 of the same priority, where task T_1 is enqueued at time N and task T_2 is enqueued at time $N + i$ $(i > 0)$, is task T_2 ever dequeued before task T_1? If so, how can you eliminate this problem and make your task scheduler fair?"

Programming Exercise 2

After removing the root data item, the remove operation moves an existing data item to the root and continues to move that data item downward until a heap is produced. The following function performs a similar task, except that the heap it is building is rooted at array entry `root` and occupies only a portion of the array.

`void moveDown ( DataType dataItem [], int root, int size )`

Requirements:
The left and right subtrees of the binary tree rooted at `root` are heaps[1]. Parameter `size` is the number of data items in the array.

Results:
Restores the binary tree rooted at `root` to a heap by moving `dataItems[root]` downward until the tree satisfies the heap property.

In this exercise, you implement an efficient sorting algorithm called heap sort using the `moveDown` function. You first use this function to transform an array into a heap. You then remove data items one-by-one from the heap (from the highest priority data item to the lowest) until you produce a sorted array.

Let's begin by examining how you transform an unsorted array into a heap. Each leaf of any binary tree is a one-data item heap. You can build a heap containing three data items from a pair of sibling leaves by applying the `moveDown` function to that pair's parent. The four single-data item heaps (leaf nodes) in the following tree

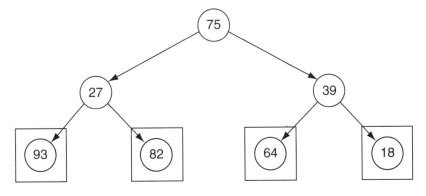

Index	Entry
0	75
1	27
2	39
3	93
4	82
5	64
6	18

are transformed by the calls `moveDown(sample,1,7)` and `moveDown(sample,2,7)` into a pair of three-data item heaps.

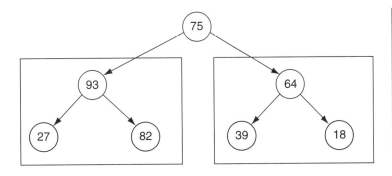

Index	Entry
0	75
1	93
2	64
3	27
4	82
5	39
6	18

---

[1]This requirement cannot be efficiently tested, so we do not throw an exception when it is not valid. Instead, we do not guarantee the correctness of the moveDown function if the requirement is not met.

By repeating this process, you build larger and larger heaps, until you transform the entire tree (array) into a heap.

```
// Build successively larger heaps within the array until the
// entire array is a heap.
for ( j = (size-1)/2 ; j >= 0 ; --j )
     moveDown(dataItems,j,size);
```

Combining the pair of three-data item heaps shown previously using the call `moveDown(sample,0,7)`, for instance, produces the following heap.

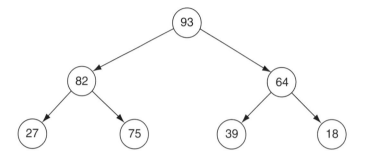

Index	Entry
0	93
1	82
2	64
3	27
4	75
5	39
6	18

Now that you have a heap, you remove data items of decreasing priority from the heap and gradually construct an array that is sorted in ascending order. The root of the heap contains the highest priority data item. If you swap the root with the data item at the end of the array and use `moveDown` to form a new heap, you end up with a heap containing six data items and a sorted array containing one data item. Performing this process a second time yields a heap containing five data items and a sorted array containing two data items.

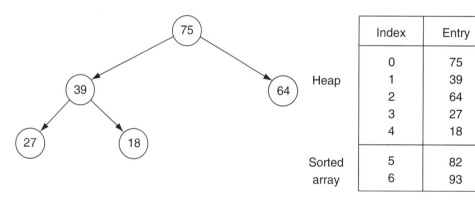

Index	Entry
0	75
1	39
2	64
3	27
4	18
5	82
6	93

You repeat this process until the heap is gone and a sorted array remains.

```
// Swap the root data item from each successively smaller heap with
// the last unsorted data item in the array. Restore the heap after
// each exchange.
for ( j = size-1 ; j > 0 ; --j )
{
    temp = dataItems[j];
    dataItems[j] = dataItems[0];
    dataItems[0] = temp;
    moveDown(dataItems,0,j);
}
```

A shell containing a `heapSort` function comprised of the two loops shown above is given in the file *heapsort.cs*.

Step 1: Using your implementation of the `remove` operation as a basis, create an implementation of the `moveDown` function.

Step 2: Add your implementation of the `moveDown` function to the shell in the file *heapsort.cs* thereby completing code needed by the `heapSort` function. Save the result in the file *heapsort.cpp*.

Step 3: Before testing the resulting `heapSort` function using the test program in the file *test11hs.cpp*, prepare Test Plan 11-3 for the `heapSort` function that covers arrays of different lengths containing a variety of priority values. Be sure to include arrays that have multiple data items with the same priority.

Step 4: Execute your test plan. If you discover mistakes in your implementation of the `moveDown` and `heapSort` functions, correct them and execute your test plan again.

Programming Exercise 3

Examining the tree form of a heap rotated ninety degrees counterclockwise from its conventional orientation can be awkward. Because a heap is a complete tree, an unambiguous representation in tree form can be generated by outputting the heap level-by-level, with each level output on a separate line.

```
void writeLevels () const
```

Requirements:
None

Results:
Outputs the data items in a heap in level order, one level per line. Only outputs each data item's priority. If the heap is empty, then outputs "Empty heap".

The first tree shown on the first page of this laboratory, for example, yields the following output.

```
93
82 64
27 75 39 18
```

Step 1: Implement this operation and add it to the file *Heap.cpp*. A prototype for this operation is included in the declaration of the Heap class in the file *Heap.h*.

Step 2: Activate test 1 (the write levels command) in the test program in the file *test11.cpp* by changing the value of LAB11_TEST1 from 0 to 1 in the *config.h* file and recompiling.

Step 3: Prepare Test Plan 11-4 for this operation that covers heaps of various sizes, including empty and single-data item heaps.

Step 4: Execute your test plan. If you discover mistakes in your implementation of the `writeLevels` operation, correct them and execute your test plan again.

Analysis Exercise 1

You can use a heap—or a priority queue (Programming Exercise 1)—to implement both a first-in, first-out (FIFO) queue and a stack. The trick is to use the order in which data items arrive as the basis for determining the data items' priority values.

Part A

How would you assign priority values to data items to produce a FIFO queue?

Part B

How would you assign priority values to data items to produce a stack?

Analysis Exercise 2

Part A

Given a heap containing ten data items with distinct priorities, where in the heap can the data item with the next-to-highest priority be located? Give examples to illustrate your answer.

Part B

Given the same heap as in Part A, where in the heap can the data item with the lowest priority be located? Give examples to illustrate your answer.

Weighted Graph ADT

In this laboratory you

- create an implementation of the Weighted Graph ADT using a vertex list and an adjacency matrix.

- develop a routine that finds the least costly (or shortest) path between each pair of vertices in a graph.

- add vertex coloring and implement a function that checks whether a graph has a proper coloring.

- investigate the Four-Color Theorem by generating a graph for which no proper coloring can be created using less than five colors.

Objectives

ADT Overview

Many relationships cannot be expressed easily using either a linear or a hierarchical data structure. The relationship between the cities connected by a highway network is one such relationship. Although it is possible for the roads in the highway network to describe a relationship between cities that is either linear (a one way street, for example) or hierarchical (an expressway and its off-ramps, for instance), we all have driven in circles enough times to know that most highway networks are neither linear nor hierarchical. What we need is a data structure that lets us connect each city to any of the other cities in the network. This type of data structure is referred to as a graph.

Like a tree, a graph consists of a set of nodes (called vertices) and a set of edges. Unlike a tree, an edge in a graph can connect any pair of vertices, not simply a parent and its child. The following graph represents a simple highway network.

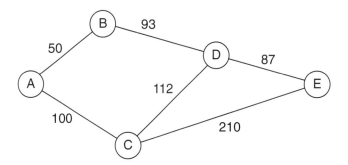

Each vertex in the graph has a unique label that denotes a particular city. Each edge has a weight that denotes the cost (measured in terms of distance, time, or money) of traversing the corresponding road. Note that the edges in the graph are undirected; that is, if there is an edge connecting a pair of vertices A and B, this edge can be used to move either from A to B, or from B to A. The resulting weighted, undirected graph expresses the cost of traveling between cities using the roads in the highway network. In this laboratory, you focus on the implementation and application of weighted, undirected graphs.

C++ Concepts Overview

Two dimensional arrays: Unfortunately, C++ does not cleanly represent dynamically sized two dimensional arrays. The two main approaches that C++ supports are 1) an array of pointers to one dimensional arrays, or 2) a one dimensional array that the programmer explicitly maps the two dimensions onto. For option one, the syntax looks like `array[row][col]`, but requires two pointer dereferences per access and extensive setup and teardown in constructors and destructors. Option two only requires a single pointer dereference, but the syntax doesn't look like a two dimensional array reference and requires extra work by the programmer for the mapping on each reference. In this lab, we chose the second option for implementation.

Weighted Graph ADT

Data Items

Each vertex in a graph has a label (of type string) that uniquely identifies it. Vertices may include additional data.

Structure

The relationship between the vertices in a graph is expressed using a set of undirected edges, where each edge connects one pair of vertices. Collectively, these edges define a symmetric relation between the vertices. Each edge in a weighted graph has a weight that denotes the cost of traversing that edge.

Operations

`WeightedGraph ( int maxNumber = MAX_GRAPH_SIZE )`

Requirements:
None

Results:
Constructor. Creates an empty graph. Allocates enough memory for a graph containing `maxNumber` vertices.

`WeightedGraph ( const WeightedGraph& other )`

Requirements:
None

Results:
Copy constructor. Initializes the weighted graph to be equivalent to the `other` weighted graph parameter.

`WeightedGraph& operator= ( const WeightedGraph& other )`

Requirements:
None

Results:
Overloaded assignment operator. Sets the weighted graph to be equivalent to the `other` weighted graph parameter and returns a reference to this object.

`~WeightedGraph ()`

Requirements:
None

Results:
Destructor. Deallocates (frees) the memory used to store a graph.

```
void insertVertex ( const Vertex& newVertex )
```

Requirements:
Graph is not full.

Results:
Inserts `newVertex` into a graph. If the vertex already exists in the graph, then updates it.

```
void insertEdge ( const string& v1, const string& v2, int wt )
                  throw ( logic_error )
```

Requirements:
Graph includes vertices `v1` and `v2`.

Results:
Inserts an undirected edge connecting vertices `v1` and `v2` into the graph. The weight of the edge is `wt`. If there is already an edge connecting these vertices, then updates the weight of the edge.

```
bool retrieveVertex ( const string& v, Vertex& vData ) const
```

Requirements:
None

Results:
Searches a graph for vertex `v`. If this vertex is found, then places the value of the vertex's data in `vData` and returns `true`. Otherwise, returns `false` with `vData` undefined.

```
bool getEdgeWeight ( const string& v1, const string& v2, int& wt )
                     const  throw ( logic_error )
```

Requirements:
Graph includes vertices `v1` and `v2`.

Results:
Searches the graph for the edge connecting vertices `v1` and `v2`. If this edge exists, then places the weight of the edge in `wt` and returns true. Otherwise, returns `false` with `wt` undefined.

```
void removeVertex ( const string& v ) throw ( logic_error )
```

Requirements:
Graph includes vertex `v`.

Results:
Removes vertex `v` from the graph and any edges connected to `v`.

✗ `void removeEdge ( const string& v1, const string& v2 )`
                    `throw ( logic_error )`

Requirements:
Graph includes vertices `v1` and `v2`.

Results:
Removes the edge connecting vertices `v1` and `v2` from the graph.

`void clear ()`

Requirements:
None

Results:
Removes all the vertices and edges in the graph.

`bool isEmpty () const`

Requirements:
None

Results:
Returns `true` if the graph is empty (no vertices). Otherwise, returns `false`.

`bool isFull () const`

Requirements:
None

Results:
Returns `true` if the graph is full (cannot add any more vertices). Otherwise, returns `false`.

`void showStructure () const`

Requirements:
None

Results:
Outputs the graph with the vertices in array form and the edges in adjacency matrix form (with their weights). If the graph is empty, outputs "Empty graph". Note that this operation is intended for testing/debugging purposes only.

Implementation Notes

Two dimensional arrays: To map a two dimensional array onto a one dimensional array (row, column) → (array index), use the following formula: *arrayIndex = row * numColumnsPerRow + column.*

You can represent a graph in many ways. In this laboratory, you use an array to store the set of vertices and an adjacency matrix to store the set of edges. An entry (*j, k*) in an adjacency matrix contains information on the edge that goes from the vertex with index *j* to the vertex with index *k*. For a weighted graph, each matrix entry contains the weight of the corresponding edge. A specially chosen weight value is used to indicate edges that are missing from the graph.

The following graph

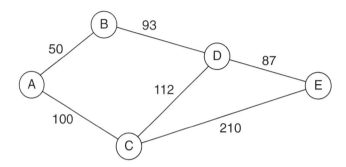

yields the vertex list and adjacency matrix shown below. A '–' is used to denote an edge that is missing from the graph.

Vertex list		Adjacency matrix					
Index	Label	From\To	0	1	2	3	4
0	A	0	–	50	100	–	–
1	B	1	50	–	–	93	–
2	C	2	100	–	–	112	210
3	D	3	–	93	112	–	87
4	E	4	–	–	210	87	–

Vertex A has an array index of 0 and vertex C has an array index of 2. The weight of the edge from vertex A to vertex C is therefore stored in entry (0, 2) in the adjacency matrix.

Step 1: Implement the operations in the Weighted Graph ADT using an array to store the vertices (`vertexList`) and an adjacency matrix to store the edges (`adjMatrix`). The number of vertices in a graph is not fixed, therefore you need to store the maximum number of vertices the graph can hold (`maxSize`) as well as the actual number of vertices in the graph (`size`). Base your implementation on the declarations from the file *WeightedGraph.h*. An implementation of the showStructure operation is given in the file *show12.cpp*.

Your implementations of the public member functions should use your getEdge and setEdge helper functions to access entries in the adjacency matrix. For example, the assignment statement

```
setEdge(2,3, 100);
```

uses the `setEdge` function to assign a weight of 100 to the entry in the second row, third column of the adjacency matrix and the following statement

```
if ( getEdge(j,k) == INFINITE_EDGE_WT )
    cout << "Edge is missing from graph" << endl;
```

uses `getEdge` to test whether there is an edge connecting the vertex with index *j* and the vertex with index *k*.

Step 2: Save your implementation of the Weighted Graph ADT in the file *WeightedGraph.cpp*. Be sure to document your code.

Compilation Directions

Compile *test12.cpp* with *WeightedGraph.cpp*. Weighted Graph is not a templated class and is not being #included by the test program.

Testing

The test program in the file *test12.cpp* allows you to interactively test your implementation of the Weighted Graph ADT using the following commands.

Command	Action
+v	Insert vertex v.
=v w wt	Insert an edge connecting vertices v and w. The weight of this edge is wt.
?v	Retrieve vertex v.
#v w	Retrieve the edge connecting vertices v and w and output its weight.
-v	Remove vertex v.
!v w	Remove the edge connecting vertices v and w.
E	Report whether the graph is empty.
F	Report whether the graph is full.
C	Clear the graph.
Q	Quit the test program.

Note that v and w denote vertex labels (type `string`) not individual characters (type `char`). As a result, you must be careful to enter these commands using the exact format shown above, including spaces.

Step 1: Download the online test plans for Lab 12.

Step 2: Prepare Test Plan 12-1 for your implementation of the Weighted Graph ADT. Your test plan should cover graphs in which the vertices are connected in a variety of ways. Be sure to include test cases that attempt to retrieve edges that do not exist or that connect nonexistent vertices.

Step 3: Execute Test Plan 12-1. If you discover mistakes in your implementation, correct them and execute your test plan again.

Programming Exercise 1

In many applications of weighted graphs, you need to determine not only whether there is an edge connecting a pair of vertices, but whether there is a path connecting the vertices. By extending the concept of an adjacency matrix, you can produce a path matrix in which an entry (j, k) contains the cost of the least costly (or shortest) path from the vertex with index j to the vertex with index k. The following graph

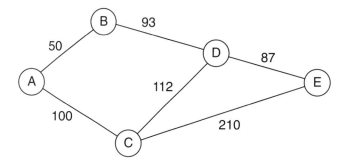

yields the path matrix shown below.

Vertex list		Path matrix					
Index	Label	From/To:	0	1	2	3	4
0	A	0	0	50	100	143	230
1	B	1	50	0	150	93	180
2	C	2	100	150	0	112	199
3	D	3	143	93	112	0	87
4	E	4	230	180	199	87	0

This graph includes a number of paths from vertex A to vertex E. The cost of the least costly path connecting these vertices is stored in entry (0, 4) in the path matrix, where 0 is the index of vertex A and 4 is the index of vertex E. The corresponding path is ABDE.

In creating this path matrix, we have assumed that a path with cost 0 exists from a vertex to itself (entries of the form (j, j)). This assumption is based on the view that traveling from a vertex to itself is a nonevent and thus costs nothing. Depending on how you intend to apply the information in a graph, you may want to use an alternate assumption.

Given the adjacency matrix for a graph, we begin construction of the path matrix by noting that all edges are paths. These one-edge-long paths are combined to form two-edge-long paths by applying the following reasoning.

```
If   there exists a path from a vertex j to a vertex m and
     there exists a path from a vertex m to a vertex k,
then there exists a path from vertex j to vertex k.
```

We can apply this same reasoning to these newly generated paths to form paths consisting of more and more edges. The key to this process is to enumerate and combine paths in a manner that is both complete and efficient. One approach to this task is described in the following algorithm, known as Warshall's algorithm. Note that variables j, k, and m refer to vertex indices, *not* vertex labels.

```
Initialize the path matrix so that it is the same as the edge
matrix (all edges are paths). In addition, create a path with
cost 0 from each vertex back to itself.
for ( m = 0 ; m < size ; ++m )
  for ( j = 0 ; j < size ; ++j )
     for ( k = 0 ; k < size ; ++k )
        If there exists a path from vertex j to vertex m and
           there exists a path from vertex m to vertex k,
        then add a path from vertex j to vertex k to the path matrix.
```

This algorithm establishes the existence of paths between vertices but not their costs. Fortunately, by extending the reasoning used above, we can easily determine the costs of the least costly paths between vertices.

```
If there exists a path from a vertex j to a vertex m and
   there exists a path from a vertex m to a vertex k and
   the cost of going from j to m to k is less than entry (j,k) in
      the path matrix,
then replace entry (j,k) with the sum of entries (j,m) and (m,k).
```

Incorporating this reasoning into the previous algorithm yields the following algorithm, known as Floyd's algorithm.

```
Initialize the path matrix so that it is the same as the edge
matrix (all edges are paths). In addition, create a path with
cost 0 from each vertex back to itself.
for ( m = 0 ; m < size ; ++m )
  for ( j = 0 ; j < size ; ++j )
     for ( k = 0 ; k < size ; ++k )
        If there exists a path from vertex j to vertex m and
           there exists a path from vertex m to vertex k and
           the sum of entries (j,m) and (m,k) is less than
           entry (j,k) in the path matrix,
        then replace entry (j,k) with the sum of entries (j,m)
              and (m,k).
```

The following Weighted Graph ADT operation displays a graph's path matrix.

```
void showShortestPaths () const
```

Requirements:
None

Results:
Computes and displays the graph's path matrix.

Step 1: Implement the showShortestPaths operation described previously and add it to the file *WeightedGraph.cpp.*

Step 2: Activate Test 1 by changing the value of LAB12_TEST1 from 0 to 1 in the *config.h* file and recompiling *test12.cpp.*

Step 3: Prepare Test Plan 12-2 for the showShortestPaths operation that includes graphs in which the vertices are connected in a variety of ways with a variety of weights. Be sure to include test cases in which an edge between a pair of vertices has a higher cost than a multiedge path between these same vertices. The edge CE and the path CDE in the graph shown on page 158 have this property.

Step 4: Execute Test Plan 12-2. If you discover mistakes in your implementation of the `showShortestPaths` operation, correct them and execute your test plan again.

Programming Exercise 2

Suppose you wish to create a road map of a particular highway network. In order to avoid causing confusion among map users, you must be careful to color the cities in such a way that no cities sharing a common border also share the same color. An assignment of colors to cities that meets this criterion is called a proper coloring of the map.

Restating this problem in terms of a graph, we say that an assignment of colors to the vertices in a graph is a proper coloring of the graph if no vertex is assigned the same color as an adjacent vertex. The assignment of colors (black and white) shown in the following graph is an example of a proper coloring.

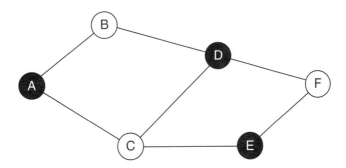

Two colors are not always enough to produce a proper coloring. One of the most famous theorems in graph theory, the Four-Color Theorem, states that creating a proper coloring of any planar graph (that is, any graph that can be drawn on a sheet of paper without having the edges cross one another) requires using at most four colors. A planar graph that requires four colors is shown below. Note that if a graph is not planar, you may need to use more than four colors.

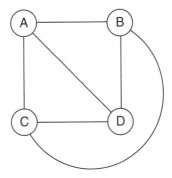

The following Weighted Graph ADT operation determines whether a graph has a proper coloring.

```
bool hasProperColoring () const
```

Requirements:
All the vertices have been assigned a color.

Results:
Returns `true` if no vertex in the graph has the same color as an adjacent vertex. Otherwise, returns `false`.

Step 1: Implement the `hasProperColoring` operation described above and add it to the file *WeightedGraph.cpp*.

Step 2: Activate Test 2 by changing the value of LAB12_TEST2 from 0 to 1 in the *config.h* file and recompiling the test program. By activating TEST2, the test program will read a vertex label *and* color when using the + operation to insert a vertex.

Step 3: Prepare Test Plan 12-3 for the `hasProperColoring` operation that includes a variety of graphs and vertex colorings.

Step 4: Execute Test Plan 12-3. If you discover mistakes in your implementation of the `hasProperColoring` operation, correct them and execute your test plan again.

Programming Exercise 3

A communications network consists of a set of switching centers (vertices) and a set of communications lines (edges) that connect these centers. When designing a network, a communications company needs to know whether the resulting network will continue to support communications between *all* centers should any one of these communications lines be rendered inoperative due to weather or equipment failure. That is, they need to know the answer to the following question.

Given a graph in which there is a path from every vertex to every other vertex, will removing any edge from the graph always produce a graph in which there is *still* a path from every vertex to every other vertex?

Obviously, the answer to this question depends on the graph. The answer for the graph shown below is yes.

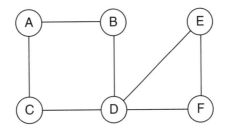

On the other hand, you can divide the following graph into two disconnected subgraphs by removing the edge connecting vertices D and E. Thus, for this graph the answer is no.

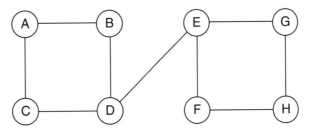

Although determining an answer to this question for an arbitrary graph is somewhat difficult, there are certain classes of graphs for which the answer is always yes. Given the definitions

- A graph G is said to be connected if there exists a path from every vertex in G to every other vertex in G,
- The degree of a vertex V in a graph G is the number of edges in G that connect to V, where an edge from V to itself counts twice,

the following rule can be derived using simple graph theory

If all of the vertices in a connected graph are of even degree, then removing any one edge from the graph will always produce a connected graph.

If this rule applies to a graph, then you know that the answer to the previous question is yes for that graph. Note that this rule tells you nothing about connected graphs in which the degree of one or more vertices is odd.

The following Weighted Graph ADT operation checks whether every vertex in a graph is of even degree.

```
bool areAllEven () const
```

Requirements:
None

Results:
Returns `true` if every vertex in a graph is of even degree. Otherwise, returns `false`.

Step 1: Implement the `areAllEven` operation described above and add it to the file *WeightedGraph.cpp*. A prototype for this operation is included in the declaration of the Weighted Graph ADT in the file *WeightedGraph.h*.

Step 2: Activate Test 3 by changing the value of LAB12_TEST3 from 0 to 1 in the *config.h* file and recompiling the test program.

Step 3: Prepare Test Plan 12-4 for this operation that includes graphs in which the vertices are connected in a variety of ways.

Step 4: Execute Test Plan 12-4. If you discover mistakes in your implementation of the `areAllEven` operation, correct them and execute your test plan again.

Analysis Exercise 1

Floyd's algorithm (see Programming Exercise 1) computes the shortest path between each pair of vertices in a graph. Suppose you need to know not only the cost of the shortest path between a pair of vertices, but also which vertices lie along this path. At first, it may seem that you need to store a list of vertices for every entry in the path matrix. Fortunately, you do not need to store this much information. For each entry (j, k) in the path matrix, all you need to know is the index of the vertex that follows j on the shortest path from j to k—that is, the index of the second vertex on the shortest path from j to k. The following graph, for example,

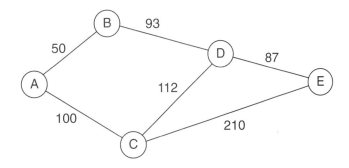

yields the augmented path matrix shown below.

Vertex list		Path matrix (cost|second vertex on shortest path)				
Index	Label	From/To	0	1	2	3	4
0	A	0	0|0	50|1	100|2	143|1	230|1
1	B	1	50|0	0|1	150|0	93|3	180|3
2	C	2	100|0	150|0	0|2	112|3	199|3
3	D	3	143|1	93|1	112|2	0|3	87|4
4	E	4	230|3	180|3	199|3	87|3	0|4

Entry (0, 4) in this path matrix indicates that the cost of the shortest path from vertex A to vertex E is 230. It further indicates that vertex B (the vertex with index 1) is the second vertex on the shortest path. Thus the shortest path is of the form AB...E.

Explain how you can use this augmented path matrix to list the vertices that lie along the shortest path between a given pair of vertices.

Analysis Exercise 2

Give an example of a graph for which no proper coloring can be created using less than five colors (see Programming Exercise 2). Does your example contradict the Four-Color Theorem?

Performance Evaluation

In this laboratory, you

- use a Timer class to measure the length of time between two events—when a function starts and when it finishes, for instance.

- compare the performance of searching and sorting routines.

- compare the performance implications of common C++ constructs.

ADT Overview

A routine's performance can be judged in many ways and on many levels. In other laboratories, you describe performance using order-of-magnitude estimates of a routine's execution time. You develop these estimates by analyzing how the routine performs its task, paying particular attention to how it uses iteration and recursion. You then express the routine's projected execution time as a function of the number of data items (N) that it manipulates as it performs its task. The results are estimates of the form $O(N)$, $O(LogN)$, and so on.

These order-of-magnitude estimates allow you to group routines based on their projected performance under different conditions (best case, worst case, average case). As important as these order-of-magnitude estimates are, they are by their very nature, high-level estimates of the amount of work that needs to be done, not how much time it will take. They do not take into account factors specific to a particular environment, such as how a routine is implemented, the hardware and operating system of the computer system on which it is being run, and the kind of data being processed. If you are to accurately determine how well or poorly a given routine will perform in a particular environment, you need to evaluate the routine in that environment.

In this laboratory, you measure the performance of a variety of routines. You begin by completing a set of tools that allow you to measure execution time. Then you use these tools to measure the execution times of the routines.

You can determine a routine's execution time in a number of ways. The timings performed in this laboratory will be generated using the approach summarized next.

Get the current system time (call this *startTime*).

Execute the routine.

Get the current system time (call this *stopTime*).

The routine's execution time = *stopTime* – *startTime*.

If the routine executes very rapidly, then the difference between *startTime* and *stopTime* may be too small for your computer system to measure. Should this be the case, you need to execute the routine multiple times and divide the length of the resulting time interval by the number of repetitions, as follows:

Get the current system time (call this *startTime*).

Execute the routine *m* times.

Get the current system time (call this *stopTime*).

The routine's execution time = (*stopTime* – *startTime*) / *m*.

To use this approach, you must have some way to read and then save the "current system time". How the current system time is defined and how it is accessed varies from system to system. Two common methods are outlined here.

Method 1

Use a function call to get the amount of processor time that your program (or process) has used. Typically the processor time is measured in clock ticks or fractions of a second. You can use this approach on most systems. You should use this approach on multiuser or multiprocess systems where the routine you are timing is not the only program running. This is what we do in our implementation of the Timer ADT.

Method 2

Use a function call to get the current time of day. Time of day is also called "wall clock" because it refers to the current real time the way a clock on the wall would measure it; using it to measure time measures the time spent in all system processes—not just the one being timed. This method may be sufficiently accurate on single-user/single-process systems where the routine you are timing is the only program running.

In addition to acquiring and storing a point in time, you also need a convenient mechanism for measuring time intervals. The Timer ADT described below uses the familiar stopwatch metaphor to describe the timing process.

Start the timer.

...

Stop the timer.

Read the elapsed time.

C++ Concepts Overview

STL: The Standard Template Library (STL) provides implementations of common data structures and algorithms. These data structures mirror many of the data structures that you have developed in this lab book. We give a brief exposure to the STL in this lab to help make you aware of the STL and to illustrate some more advanced C++ coding techniques. For general use, we recommend that you use the STL unless there is a compelling reason not to, such as when working on an old system that does not support the STL.

Overloading pre- vs. post-increment operators: Both the pre- and post-increment operators can be overloaded. Both are unary operators with the same name (operator++), but a slightly different signature so that the compiler knows which one to use. They require different implementations to achieve their semantics properly. One of the learning goals of this lab is to discover that the difference between the two operators is not just a matter of semantics, but also that the performance of the two operators can differ significantly.

Templated functions: In addition to using templates to create entire generic classes, we can use the template facility to create generic functions. This is useful when you want the same functionality in one function for different data types.

C preprocessor: Sometimes typing in everything the compiler needs to see unnecessarily complicates the code, making it more difficult to write correctly and harder to understand. We use some preprocessor magic—inherited from C—to improve the code legibility. We use #define in *constructor.cpp* to clean up a complicated function call.

Function pointers: C++ supports the ability to use a pointer to reference functions, not just data. Dereferencing function pointers results in the execution of the referenced code. This advanced feature is very powerful and was initially used to implement many aspects of object oriented programming—such as inheritance and polymorphism—in C++ compilers.

Timer ADT

Data Items
A pair of values that denote the beginning and length of a time interval.

Structure
None

Operations

`Timer ()`

Requirements:
None

Results:
Constructor. Initializes the internal timer values so that the timer is ready to measure time.

`void start () throw ( runtime_error )`

Requirements:
The `clock` function is working correctly.

Results:
Marks the beginning of a time interval (starts the timer).

`void stop () throw ( logic_error )`

Requirements:
The beginning of a time interval has been marked.

Results:
Marks the end of a time interval (stops the timer).

`double getElapsedTime () const throw ( logic_error )`

Requirements:
The beginning and end of a time interval have been marked.

Results:
Returns the length of the time interval in seconds.

Implementation Notes

The start operation is the only operation in the lab book that throws an exception other than `logic_error`. We do this because the exception would come from an error in the system—not in the ADT or parameters to the function. Therefore, the exception is not a logical error, but a runtime error.

Noticing the runtime error illustrates an important systems programming concept: checking the error status of system calls. The clock function that C++ provides returns an error value of –1 when it doesn't work correctly. By checking for this errant value, we ensure that we don't continue a timing operation when we have no way of getting a meaningful time from the system. We throw an error to let the programmer using the ADT decide how to proceed.

Step 1: Select one of the two methods for acquiring and representing a point in time and use this method to create an implementation of the Timer ADT. Base your implementation on the class declaration from the file *Timer.h*.

Step 2: Save your implementation of the Timer ADT in the file *Timer.cpp*.

Step 3: Determine the resolution of your implementation. That is, what is the shortest time interval it can accurately measure? You must determine the correct way to report the CPU usage in seconds.

Compilation Directions

When measuring the performance of your routines, you must tell the compiler to generate efficient code. By default, most compilers generate machine code that is similar to the C++ code you write. Usually, this is not the fastest way to execute on a machine. Instead, you should use a "compiler flag" that directs the compiler to generate the most efficient machine code it can. Ask your instructor for directions on how to perform this for your compiler.

Testing

Step 1: Write a test program that allows you to test the accuracy of your implementation of the Timer ADT by measuring time intervals of known duration. Our implementation of the timer returns different values based on the operating system

Step 2: Compile your implementation of the Timer ADT in the file *Timer.cpp* and the test program in the file *test13.cpp*.

Step 3: Prepare Test Plan 13-1 for your implementation of the Timer ADT. Your test plan should cover intervals of various lengths, including intervals at or near the resolution of your implementation.

Step 4: Execute your test plan. If you discover mistakes in your implementation, correct them and execute your test plan again.

Measurement and Analysis Exercise 1

In this exercise, you examine the performance of the searching routines in the file *search.cpp*.

Step 1: Use the program in the file *search.cpp* to measure the execution times of the linearSearch, binarySearch, and STLSearch classes.

This program begins by generating an ordered list of integer keys (keyList) and a set of keys to search for in this list (searchSet). It then measures the amount of time it takes to search for the keys using the specified routines and computes the average time per search.

The constant numRepetitions controls how many times each search is executed. Depending on the speed of your system, you may need to use a value of numRepetitions that differs from the value given in the test program. **Before continuing, experiment or check with your instructor to determine the value of** numRepetitions **you should use in order to obtain meaningful timing data.**

Step 2: Fill in Timings Table 13-2 with the observed execution times of the linearSearch, binarySearch, and STLSearch routines for each combination of the three test categories and the three values of numKeys listed in the table.

Step 3: Plot your results in a spreadsheet. The resulting graph should show time in seconds on the *Y* axis vs. the number of items in the list on the *X* axis. Submit the graph as directed by your instructor.

Step 4: Fill in your answer to Question 1 on the Analysis Exercise 1 worksheet: "How well do your measured times conform to the order-of-magnitude estimates given for the linearSearch and binarySearch routines?"

Step 5: Fill in your answer to Question 2 on the Analysis Exercise 1 worksheet: "Using the code in the file *search.cpp* and your measured execution times as a basis, develop an order-of-magnitude estimate of the execution time of the STLSearch routine. Briefly explain your reasoning behind this estimate."

Measurement and Analysis Exercise 2

In this exercise, you examine the performance of the set of sorting routines in the file *sort.cpp*.

Step 1: Use the program in the file *sort.cpp* to measure the execution times of the selectionSort, quickSort, and STL sort routines.

This program begins by generating a list of integer keys (keyList). It then measures the amount of time it takes to sort this list into ascending order using the specified routine.

The constant numRepetitions controls how many times each sort is executed. Depending on the speed of your system, you may need to use a value of numRepetitions that differs from the value given in the test program. **Before continuing, experiment or check with your instructor to determine the value of** numRepetitions **in** *sort.cpp* **you should use in order to obtain meaningful timing data.**

Step 2: Fill in Timings Table 13-3 with the observed execution times of the selectionSort, quickSort, and STL Sort routines for each combination of the three test categories and the three values of numKeys listed in the table.

Step 3: Plot your results in a spreadsheet. The resulting graph should show time in seconds on the *Y* axis vs. the number of items in the list on the *X* axis. Submit the graph as directed by your instructor.

Step 4: Fill in your answer to Question 1 on the Analysis Exercise 2 worksheet: "How well do your measured times conform with the order-of-magnitude estimates given for the selectionSort and quickSort routines?"

Step 5: Fill in your answer to Question 2 on the Analysis Exercise 2 worksheet: "Using the code in the file *sort.cpp* and your measured execution times as a basis, develop an order-of-magnitude estimate of the execution time of the STL sort routine. Briefly explain your reasoning behind this estimate.

Measurement and Analysis Exercise 3

In this exercise, you measure the performance of common C++ actions. We are going to explore the performance implications of different ways of using constructors and increment operators in this lab.

Step 1: The program in *constructor.cpp* lets you test the performance implications of putting a constructor inside a `for` loop versus just prior to the loop. Compile *constructor.cpp*, *Timer.cpp*, and *TestVector.cpp* together to generate a test program.

Step 2: Using the program that you generated in Step 1, measure the time it takes to construct/initialize `int`, `double`, `vector`, and `TestVector` both just prior to and inside a loop. Record the results in Table 13-4.

Step 3: Fill in your answer to Question 1 on the Analysis Exercise 3 worksheet: "For each data type, how do your measured times for the constructor just before the loop compare to the times for the constructor inside the loop? What might explain any observed differences?"

Step 4: The program in *increment.cpp* lets you test the performance implications of the post-increment operator compared with the pre-increment operator. Compile *increment.cpp*, *Timer.cpp*, and *TestVector.cpp* together to generate a test program.

Step 5: Using the program that you generated in Step 4, measure the times recorded for the pre-increment and post-increment tests for `int`, `double`, and `TestVector`. Record the results in Table 13-5.

Step 6: Fill in your answer to Question 2 on the Analysis Exercise 3 worksheet: "For each data type, how do your measured times for the pre-increment operator compare to the times for the post-increment operator? What might explain any observed differences?"

Analysis Exercise 1

You are given another pair of searching routines. Both routines have order-of-magnitude execution time estimates of $O(N)$. When you measure the actual execution times of these routines on a given system using a variety of different data sets, you discover that one routine consistently executes five times faster than the other. How can both routines be $O(N)$, yet have different execution times when they are compared using the same system and the same data?

Analysis Exercise 2

Why might the authors of the STL choose a search implementation that has the big-O performance that you observed?